THE
PRACTICAL
CANDYMAKING
COOKBOOK

with photographs by the author

Paul Villiard

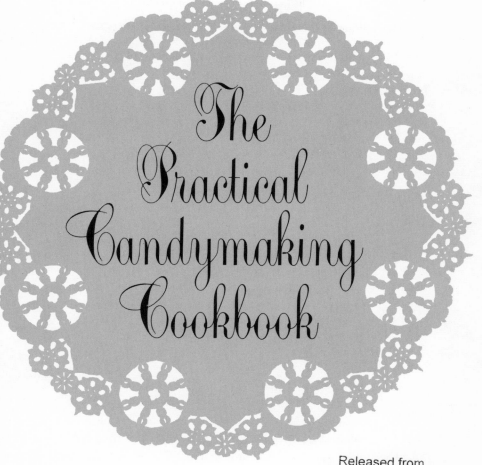

The Practical Candymaking Cookbook

ABELARD-SCHUMAN
New York   Toronto   London

LONDON	NEW YORK	TORONTO
Abelard-Schuman	Abelard-Schuman	Abelard-Schuman
Limited	Limited	Canada Limited
8 King St. WC2	257 Park Ave. So.	228 Yorkland Blvd.

An Intext Publisher

Printed in the United States of America

For Gertrude

CONTENTS

ACKNOWLEDGMENTS

I would like to take this opportunity to extend my thanks to the great number of people responsible for helping me in the past few years to assemble the knowledge that made this book possible. Many persons and companies contribute to putting a book together—furnishing supplies, equipment, and giving answers to questions—these are just a few of the ways an author is helped in his work.

In particular I would like to thank:

The Best Foods Division of Corn Products Company for supplies and for certain recipes that they contributed.

The Barth Vitamin Corporation of Valley Stream, New York for diet and health materials, and also for some recipes for diet candies.

Mrs. Mildred Arthur of Glen Rock, New Jersey for the use of a few of her recipes for low-calorie candies.

Thomas Mills Manufacturing Company, 1301 North 8th Street, Philadelphia, Pennsylvania for supplying equipment and advice.

Polak's Frutal Works Inc., of Middletown, New York, who supplied me with samples of their line of excellent candy flavors and essential oils.

To my unseen and unsung editor, whose patience and understanding made the work go so much more smoothly than it might have without his help, I offer my special regards.

And I would be remiss if I did not mention the Honeywell Photographic Company of Denver, Colorado, who very generously supplied me with the equipment used in taking the photographic illustrations for this book. A Honeywell Spotmatic camera equipped with an Auto/660 Strobonar electronic light and a Super-Takumar Macro lens were used exclusively.

ABOUT THIS BOOK

This is a story book.

It is the story of how to make fine candy in your own home kitchen. The candy described, however, is not like any candy you have made prior to this. It is fine, professional candy, but of a quality that a person may encounter only once or twice in a lifetime!

This volume is not written as a text book, or even the usual kind of cookbook, in which you turn the page to a recipe, and use it, then close the book. It *is* a story book, and I will carry you through the unfamiliar technicalities of this fine, professional candymaking, in your own kitchen just as if we were speaking together.

I have made all the different kinds of candies in this book for nearly 50 years. By now I could very nearly make them in my sleep. But—the thing I keep in mind constantly, is that *you* have not made this candy, and even wide awake *you* cannot make it, if I do not remember every single movement in the process and tell it to you in a language you can understand.

In many cookbooks, as in many other how-to-do books, the mistake the writer makes is to assume *some* knowledge of the process on the part of the reader. I am going to try not to make that mistake. I am assuming that you know nothing whatever about candymaking, that you are a veritable tyro of the kitchen range.

Right about now, you are exclaiming that this is ridiculous. That certainly you know how to make candy—why, your "fudge was the best that the church bazaar ever had, last spring." Maybe it was, but fudge is not what we are teaching you to make in this book, (even though there *is* a recipe for fudge later on). What we are going to do is make a candymaker out of you. A whole new concept of cooking, a new skill, the products of which will command your joy and satisfaction, and the envy of everyone who knows you.

And so, when I tell you again and again, little details that you think are redundant, bear with me. These redundant details are the ones that you are usually *assumed* to know, but which can be the very detail that can trip you up and make your work a failure, maybe simply because you *didn't* know them.

Do not be afraid that the work I will outline for you will be so technical that you will be unable to perform it. It is technical, but I have reduced the technicalities to ordinary household routines, the professional measurements to cups, spoonfuls and ordinary ounces and pounds. Certainly there will be a number of technical terms and words, the meanings of which may be obscure to you at first, but these words will be found in a glossary at the end of the book, explained so that you can understand them.

Please do not think that, by way of all this explanation, I am trying to "write down" to you. I am not. I am, by using simple, conversational language, opening a whole new world to you in food preparation. An exciting and satisfying new world, because now, in your own kitchen, with the few simple and easy-to-use tools required, you will be able to make such professional goodies as cordialled cherries—(do you know how to get the juice inside the chocolate coatings?)—flower-flavored French Creams that are positively addictive, they are so good, and which are practically *never* found in stores in the United States, and many, many more wonderful things, heretofore beyond the ability of the home cook.

—PAUL VILLIARD

Saugerties, New York
May, 1970

THE
PRACTICAL
CANDYMAKING
COOKBOOK

Part One

How to make
professional kinds
of candies
in the
home kitchen

The World of Candies

The desire for something sweet is an ancient one. Records found in tombs 4000 years old show the making of candy and of other kinds of sweetmeats. There is no doubt but that candy was first eaten because it tasted good, in recent times it has been proven that candy is an important item of food. It is a source of high and quick energy. It is easy to digest. It is an important control item in certain biological conditions of man.

There are records of confectioners in the tombs of such famous figures as Tutankhamen, and Rameses, some of them even giving directions for the making of candy from honey, sweet herbs and seeds. Sugar was unknown at that time, and the main sweetening ingredient was honey, which was hardened, either by cooking with fire, or by sun drying. Honey was thickened by the addition of starch or seeds to the point where it could be handled and cut into manageable pieces. Fruits were candied in honey, sometimes being rolled in toasted sesame seeds to cover the outside with a non-sticky layer.

In the last few centuries before Christ, sugar cane was known and grown for the extraction of its sweet sap. The plant, one of the grasses, was known to Alexander the Great and, later, to the Crusaders, who found the source of sugar in Asia. Since that time sugar cane has been carried by explorers completely around the world, samples being planted in most of the tropical countries, even in the southern part of the United States.

Until the discovery of sugar, candy was only accessible to the very rich—princes, kings and rulers. It is not known exactly where the refining of sugar from the juice of the cane was discovered. Probably it was in China, or possibly in Arabia. Certainly, the word candy is derived from the Arabian word *quand,* meaning sugar. Records show that as early as the seventh century the Chinese were producing a very crude kind of sugar from sugar cane. The Egyptians and the Arabs were probably the first peoples to refine sugar into some semblance of the crystallized product with which we are familiar today.

After sugar in its crude form—molded into huge "loaves" and wrapped in leaves—was introduced into Europe, Italy (specifically the city of Venice) became the European center, and thus the world center, of sugar work. The Venetians were the first to re-refine sugar again and again until they purified it into fine uniform crystals. They proceded to develop the art of sugar sculpture by molding the refined product into all imaginable kinds of intricate forms, until the city became known as the sugar capital of Europe.

Christopher Columbus took cuttings of sugar cane with him on his voyages of discovery, to plant in the New World. Sugar refineries appeared in many of the lush tropical countries where sugar cane grew. It was the increasing availability of sugar that contributed the greatest impetus to the development of candymaking.

Once it was discovered that sugar chemistry was complex, and that by different treatments of the product, different results could be obtained, it was merely a matter of experimentation by interested investigators to create the many kinds of confections with which we are still familiar.

Chemically, sugar is composed of carbon, hydrogen and oxygen. It is not only obtained from sugar cane, but may also come from sugar beets, sugar maple trees, certain palm trees and from a few other sources. Since sugar cane is the largest main source of sugar and, since the plant thrives best in hot, damp countries, it soon became the main crop in the West Indies, and later, in the Hawaiian Islands and the Philippines. Refineries, however, were established in the industrial cities of Europe and the United States, which were then merely British colonies.

Traders, therefore, exchanged the trade goods of Europe in the Indies for crude sugar, which, in turn, was carried to the cities where the refineries converted the loaves into useable cane sugar. In this country, Philadelphia, New York and Boston were the leading cities in the sugar refining and, as a consequence, were among the first cities to harbor confectioners.

To candymakers, chocolate was only an exotic material from which a good-tasting beverage could be brewed; it was still unknown as a coating material. Most of the early candies were made by boiling sugar to high temperatures, at which point it would crystallize into a hard, glassy material that could be colored and flavored with spices and herbs. When, in the middle of the nineteenth century, candymaking machines were developed, mostly in France and in Austria, the way was opened for the mass production of candy in uniform sizes and shapes. These machines gave rise to the development of the marvellous "penny candies" of the late 1800's and the early twentieth century. Many of us still can remember the fantastic variety displayed in the candy stores of the early years of this century. Here a child could spend an hour, gazing at tray after tray, or jar after jar of the most enticing kinds of candy—all to be bought for a cent.

It was around this same time that the dietary value of candy became known. As soon as candy was recognized as an energy food, soldiers were given it to use in their campaigns. Candy was easy to carry, light in weight, gave them far more energy than did the staple foods of the times, and above all, it tasted good. One half-million pounds of candy were sent to the British army fighting the Boer War, and many tons were shipped by the United States to our armies in the Philippines and elsewhere.

With its recognition as a real food, candymaking had a drastic increase in manufacture. With the advent of World War I, the manufacture of candy bars stepped up to a new high. Candy became a valuable part of the government rations delivered to troops, and the doughboys in Europe clamored for more and more candy.

The invention of one-cent, two-cent, five-cent and ten-cent candy bars burgeoned, and the development of machines to make them in great quantities kept pace. I believe it was Mr.

Curtis, of "Baby Ruth" bar fame, who first said, "The man who develops a good candy bar, is automatically a millionaire!" And, this statement was very nearly true. While the wholesale value of candy manufactured in this country at the middle of the last century was about three million dollars, at the beginning of this century, it was closer to *half a billion* dollars, and today is considerably in excess of *three billion dollars!* This is the cost of manufacturing—not the retail value; that would be closer to *ten* billion dollars! By World War II, this country was manufacturing nearly three billion pounds of candy annually, and could not fill the demand. This necessitated importing, in addition to its fantastic manufactured output, nearly 46 million additional pounds.

The consumption of candy in the United States in 1944 reached 20.5 pounds per capita! Naturally, this is an average figure. Many persons did not consume nearly that amount, and others, far more than the average figure, but per capita consumption is based on the gross number of pounds divided by the census figure of the country. It still comes to a lot of candy consumed within one year.

Diet-conscious articles notwithstanding, candy is *not* the dire and dangerous weight-adding material it is often made out to be. Candy certainly is fattening if eaten to excess but so is meat, so are vegetables, and so is any one of the nearly 2000 items of food used by the human animal.

If a person sits down next to a box of candy and keeps dipping into it until he has consumed the entire box, it will only be a matter of a few short weeks or months before he finds his bathroom scales to be less than adequate. Candy, however, is not intended for marathon consumption. It is an occasion food, an energy food, a dessert food, not a staple article of the diet. In this context it is an important food and one that, used as it should be, gives much more pleasure than meat and potatoes, and does not unduly increase your avoirdupois!

The reason we keep saying that candy is an energy food is simple. Not all people are aware of the fact that everything taken as food must first be converted to sugar before it is utilized by the body. Certain items of food take much longer to convert than do others. Fats and fatty foods, for example, must be subjected to a long, complex chemical treatment before they are finally broken down into the sugars that the human body can assimilate. Candy, on the other hand, is already sugar. In the cooking of it, much of that sugar has been converted to invert sugars which are immediately available as food for our digestive systems. Hence, if you are tired from a strenuous day's work, from overexertion, or from lack of sleep, a piece or two of candy will perk you up so rapidly that it may amaze you. It quickly replenishes the body's natural sugars in the bloodstream and gives you a great boost. Yet it does so in a natural way, not in a narcotic or medicinal manner, as do "pep" pills.

If you are going on a long drive, for example, where you will have to be behind the wheel for a day, or more, a few pieces of candy, or a few candy bars on the seat next to you will "refuel" your body, in exactly the same way a measure of gasoline refuels your car engine. If you consume a piece of candy between the stops for meals, you will find, at the end of your drive, that you are much less exhausted than you usually were after a similar trip. The same goes for people working at strenuous jobs. If they take a "candy break" once or twice during the day, it will do much more for them than more frequent coffee breaks. The body will have a new burst of energy to go on.

In the first four decades of this century, candymaking, in Europe, rose to a high degree of skill and craftsmanship. France, Switzerland and Germany perhaps led in the manufacture of fine, handmade Chocolate Creams. There were also some very fine confectioners in England. Strangely enough, in the United States we followed a different trend—toward the mass production of hard candy, candy bars, machine-made Chocolate Creams and penny candies. Naturally, there were a few fine confectioners in the United States, but the really fine candies were generally imported from Europe as a rare, one-time treat, rather than the usual thing.

Belgium became known as the center of crystallized items for use in candymaking and for the bakery trade. There they made such exotic things as candied rose petals, violet petals, mimosa blossoms and spearmint leaves. All were edible, being used as garnishes, either on top of certain flavors of fine Chocolate Creams, or in among the chocolates after they were packed in fancy boxes. Switzerland and Holland became the centers of fine chocolate production, and Dutch chocolate, Dutch cocoa and Swiss chocolate are still the finest that can be found.

Great lengths were taken in France to embellish the individual creams, and "Fine French Creams" became the title of this kind of candy imported from that country. The creams were always handmade—meaning that the fondant centers were rolled by hand, coated by hand and decorated by hand. While in this country we were perfecting the machines (invented in France, to be sure) to make Chocolate Creams in great quantities and entirely automatically, in Europe the confections were still the products of individual craftsmen. Whole sets of flavor and decoration combinations were developed in the making of French Creams. The use of certain nuts with certain flavors became so standardized that even today, an individual confectioner rarely even thinks of using anything but pecans with orange-flavored creams, or English walnuts with vanilla. These combinations became practically mandatory. Certainly other nuts might taste as well with one flavor or another, but we cling to the traditions, as I shall be doing in this book.

The second event of great importance to the art of making candy, came with the development of chocolate. Chocolate is obtained from the beans (or nuts) of the cacao tree. This tree grows best in the hot equatorial countries and has, since the times of the Spanish conquistadors, been transplanted around the entire equatorial belt of the world. The beans grow in large, melon-like pods, which spring directly from the trunk of the tree without benefit of twig or branch.

The name chocolate is derived from the Mayan word *choqui,* meaning hot, and the word *latle,* meaning water. The beverage was made by stirring the ground chocolate beans into hot water, sweetening the concoction with honey (later, in Spain, with sugar), and flavoring it with vanilla taken from the bean of an orchid. While the earliest use of chocolate remains obscure, we do know that the Spanish conquerors were given chocolate to drink when they invaded the Mayan countries. It is alleged that Montezuma drank nothing but chocolate, and drank it only once from a goblet fashioned from virgin gold that was tossed into a lake after its use by the emperor.

However true this fanciful tale may be, it is known that the Spaniards took chocolate back to their native country with them and that the beverage became a favorite one in Spain. The

Spanish people attempted to keep the product secret and did, in fact, succeed for a time. Its introduction to Spain is attributed to Hernando Cortez. Certainly, the use of chocolate was confined to royalty, and it was through the royal families of Europe that the news of the wonderful material was spread, since for a considerable time, chocolate was so costly a beverage that only royalty could afford it. It was not until the late 1600's or the early 1700's that it came into general use and then it was still fairly expensive, and classed as a luxury drink. Consider the fact that the entire stock was about twenty-five pounds of cacao beans, in the whole of one *country* manufacturing chocolate then! Now consider the fact that in the United States alone, the *daily* consumption is well in excess of two million pounds! No wonder a sizeable sum was paid for a cup of the new and exotic beverage, to which was attributed many exotic possibilities. Chocolate was thought to be an aphrodisiac, to supply strength and stamina in warriors; it was used in religious ceremonies in the Americas from whence it originated. Even Samuel Pepys mentions in his famous Diary that he used chocolate to settle his stomach in the morning.

Chocolate, like sugar, has come to be recognized as an excellent food. It is high in protein, carbohydrates, vegetable oils and minerals. Chocolate bars now form a standard addition to every ration of the armed forces, a four-ounce bar of chocolate serving as a complete emergency meal. It is known that a diet of chocolate alone can sustain life and give energy for a considerable length of time.

In the United States, and, I suppose in other countries, too, candy is divided into three categories: boxed goods, i.e., chocolate creams, bonbons etc.; candy bars; and bulk candies, such as hard candies which are most often sold around the holidays. In this country, box candies are overwhelmingly machine-made, not handmade.

With the increasing emancipation of the American woman and her entry more and more into the areas of business, technology and industry, the trend has been away from home cooking and home doing, toward the packaged foods, prepared meals and instant foods. With the fashions following a slimming trend for the past couple of decades, the average girl is under the mistaken impression that if she even touches a candy bar, she will begin to bulge out like a tub of lard. What is more unfortunate is, that, if a girl does want to make some candy for some special treat, she will be limited today in her possibilities.

Except in a few homes scattered sparsely throughout the country, gone are the times when, of a blustery winter's evening, the entire family would gather in the kitchen and, amid shouts of laughter and much clattering of pots and pans, hold a taffy pull. Or the mother, spending an afternoon alone, with a mysterious smile on her face, would turn out a plateful of delightful gay puffs of divinity, sugary pecan pralines or some other old-fashioned confection.

Fortunately, the art of fine candymaking is not lost. It is just forgotten by all but a few. Let us hope that this book will jog the memories of some, and open the way for a new experience for many others. It can be used, not only as a home-treat source, but also as a way to make a bit of pin money, as an easy and distinctive hobby that can be most useful when a contribution to a church bazaar or a club sale is expected.

A Few Tools for Professional Results

With a few exceptions, the tools used in candymaking are usually found in any well-equipped kitchen. A large kettle, a double boiler, wooden spoons, rubber spatulas, measuring cups and spoons, should all be available. The exceptions are a few tools used specifically in candymaking, and these must be purchased from kitchen supply houses, confectioners' supply houses or bakers' suppliers. Some of the items can be found in department stores.

Of prime importance is a candy thermometer. The Taylor Company makes a "household" type of candy- and jelly-making thermometer which can be used for the purpose. It is a little short for a really large kettle, and the scale does not run as high as a professional thermometer, but it is a good tool and for most things will suffice. A copper candy thermometer with a removable scale for ease in cleaning can be purchased from confectioners' and bakers' suppliers. This is the type that is used in all the factories. It is designed to indicate the high temperatures associated with many professional and commercial candies—hard candy, lollipops and similar sorts.

Next in order of importance is a piece of marble. While several kinds of candy can be made *without* a marble slab, if you want to make any chocolate creams, hard candies or bonbons, the marble is a must. This need not be a difficult thing to obtain. There are marble yards in almost every city of any size, and a piece of plain white marble, one inch thick and 30 inches by 48 inches, is only a matter of a few dollars. Or a marble top from an old dresser can be used. The above size limits you somewhat to small batches of candy, but on the other hand, it is portable, can be placed on the kitchen table when in use and stored at the back of a convenient closet when the candymaking is completed. Even more useful, of course, would be a slab of marble cut to the same size as the top of your kitchen table, placed on it and left in place. You will, once you have had a kitchen table topped with marble, wonder how you managed without it all these years! It is fine to eat on, using place mats. Spills are wiped off with a swipe of a cloth. For making bread, pies, cakes and cookies it is a dream, for you can work right on the surface, wiping it clean after using. You can roll out a pie crust directly on the marble, with no need of rolling boards or cloths. Any kind of food preparation is much easier on a marble slab. Marble yards will cut a marble to size for you, usually while you wait. The best kinds of marbles for candymaking are Tennessee, Georgia and Vermont, none of which are expensive. It need not be polished, but it should have the surface smoothly honed. Polished marble, in addition to costing more, cannot be used for fondant making.

Other tools used for special kinds of candies are: rubber molds, obtainable from confectioners' supply houses, together with a depositing funnel and stick. This last is used to deposit Cream Wafers and Chocolate Wafers, to fill the cavities of the rubber molds, and for many other purposes.

A fondant knife, or spatula, is necessary for working fondant on the marble slab. This looks like a very wide putty knife, which can be used, in fact, if you get a certain style. First, the blade must be completely stiff and rigid. Next, the blade should run clear through the handle, not be just a tine inserted into the handle. (In the latter type of construction, you stand better than a good chance of snapping off the blade when working a stiff batch of fondant, losing the blade in the fondant, perhaps burning your knuckles in the process, and, incidently, losing the batch of candy since, unless you have a spare knife at hand, the batch will crystallize before you can recover the blade.) Paint stores and large hardware stores, as well as bakery and confectioners' supply houses, sell these kinds of spatulas. It would be

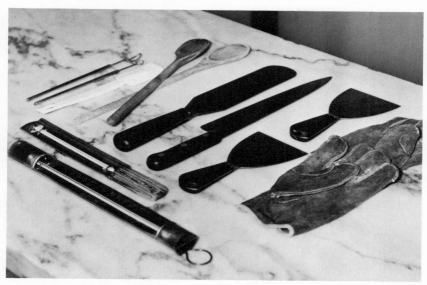

These are the essential tools needed for candymaking.

best to get two. A spare knife is always a great convenience.

At first, when learning to work up the fondant, you will probably get it all over the slab, the table, floor and yourself! It can be cleaned up very easily, but meanwhile, you must keep working the fondant to save it and keep it from returning to sugar crystals, working under a handicap much like that of a fly stuck on a piece of flypaper. The spare knife does wonders. It can be held in your other hand to keep the knife you are working with cleaned off; it can be used as a dike to stop the fondant from running off the edge of the marble; or an assistant can stand by with the spare knife, catching spills and flopping them back into the center of the marble for you. The excitement of working fondant will be demonstrated later on, and you will agree that two fondant knives *are* better than one.

Bonbon dipping forks are needed if you intend to make these highly decorative, festive candies. These can be made either by yourself, if you are something of a handyman, or purchased at a confectioners' supply house, from large kitchenware departments in fine department stores, or from any of the many mail-order companies' catalogs of gadgets.

A bonbon fork is simple: It consists of a handle of brass or copper tubing about ¼ inch in diameter and six inches long, with a loop of heavy copper wire soldered into one end. The copper wire is bent into an oblong loop about ½ inch by ¾ inch long, the two ends of the wire twisted together after forming the loop, and the twist stuck into the tubing handle and securely soldered in place. A shank of the twisted wire about two inches long is left sticking out of the handle. The loop is bent into a slight curve which, in use, cups the bonbon center as it is dipped, and makes the distinctive crown on the top of the candy when it is deposited on the paper.

A few other tools and pieces of equipment are used for making special kinds of candies, and these will be discussed in the pages dealing with the making of those items; however, there are certain supplies which are used extensively in candymaking that should be brought to your attention here.

Dipping paper is a certain kind of heavy, buff-colored paper, with one side lacquered to an extremely high gloss. This paper, used for depositing dipped chocolates, permits the chocolates to be snapped cleanly off the paper, leaving a high gloss on their bottoms. Waxed paper may be used but every once in a while the waxing, which varies from batch to batch, may sometimes either melt out from under the candy or not be thick enough in the first place, and either the bottom is pulled off the Chocolate Cream or a piece of paper is stuck to the bottom as it is lifted off. The professional dipping papers are sold by bakers' and confectioners' supply houses, in packages of 100 sheets for a reasonable sum. They can be used over and over again, as long as care is taken not to scratch the glossy surface.

Another item which will be used almost every time you make candy is the crinkled paper candy cup. These are sold in the same places as dipping papers, and come in many sizes. Size 5 is the average, and you should have white ones as well as brown. They are sold in boxes of 10,000 or 25,000. This might seem like an astronomical figure to you, but it really is not. You will be surprised to see how fast candy cups are used up. The cups are packed in sections of about 25 cups to a stack, and you slip them apart one at a time as you use them. It is easy to slip two at a time, so spin the edges of the stack to loosen the sides of the cups before you try to slip them.

Whenever Chocolate Creams are served or packed in boxes, or even packed in large boxes for storage, they should be put into individual candy cups. These serve two purposes—to keep the candies from rubbing against each other and spoiling the appearance, and to afford a neat clean way to handle the pieces. Crinkled cups made of foil are also available. These are used for very fancy candy cups, generally filled with milk or sweet chocolate with some kind of center. These cups are sold by the hundred or thousand, mostly imported from Belgium.

A Little About Chocolate

In order to be used as a covering for candy, chocolate must be "tempered." Before I start telling you how to temper the chocolate, let's discuss some of the properties of the material.

As stated earlier, chocolate is the product of the cacao tree. There are a great many different species of cacao, some of them better than others. Some of the qualities of the trees are biological. Some species are more resistant to disease, blight or weather conditions than are other species. But some species differ qualitatively as well. Some cacao beans have a better flavor after processing than do others. As a result, throughout the many years of experimentation with chocolate, each processing company has arrived at what it thinks is the best blend of different kinds of beans for its own product.

To process chocolate, the beans are roasted, then the hulls are cracked and removed. The beans are then ground into fine powder and this is put through hydraulic presses to remove most of the cocoa butter. This is a fatty substance found in cacao in quantities up to over 50% of the weight of the beans themselves.

The cakes resulting from the pressing operation are reground, sometimes several times, and subjected to further processing, ending up as the cakes of chocolate we buy as coating, or enrobing chocolate. The cocoa butter is used in many different ways, both in foods and in medicines.

Cocoa—the powder from which your breakfast drink is made—is prepared by a slightly different process, which we need not go into in this book, since our use of cocoa powder is extremely limited, used, in fact, for flavoring only one kind of chocolate cream.

Chocolate, as it is supplied to the ultimate consumer, is somewhat temperamental as to temperatures and moisture. It shows its reaction to either of these conditions by becoming streaky and gray. Chocolate will streak if it has been subjected to too high a temperature while melting, or if excessive moisture has been added, either intentionally or by accident.

If chocolate is subjected to temperatures in excess of about 140°F. it will coagulate. This is especially true of milk chocolate, which is even more temperamental than the dark chocolates.

Chocolate, as we use it for coatings, comes in three different grades:

BITTER CHOCOLATE, or "liquor," as it is called in the supply houses. This is about the same kind of chocolate as the familiar Baker's cooking chocolate you can purchase in the grocery stores. In fact, if you have difficulty in locating a good source of supply for your chocolate, you may use Baker's chocolate in place of the professional liquor. It will cost only a little more.

SWEET CHOCOLATE, or "vanilla-sweet" as it is usually called. This chocolate is the one most used for coating Chocolate Creams, and it is sweet enough for some people to be eaten as is. Personally, I find vanilla-sweet coating still too bitter for my taste.

MILK CHOCOLATE is a material familiar to everyone. Hershey bars, Nestle bars, chocolate kisses, the molded figures such as those of the Easter bunny or Santa Claus sold in candy stores, bakeries and elsewhere at holiday times—all are molded of milk chocolate. This chocolate is very sweet and tastes good. There are different grades in all three of these coating chocolates, and I would like to impress upon you now that with every single ingredient you use for candymaking, you should buy nothing but the *very best quality* you can find. This is *especially* true of chocolate.

NOTE: Some brands of chocolate coating, purchased in ten-pound cakes, have the tempering instructions printed on the paper wrapper. Where this is the case, please follow *those* directions, instead of the ones I will give you here. The reason I tell you this is that those chocolate coatings which do have the tempering instructions on the wrapper may have something a little different about them, as compared to regular coating. By this I do not mean to imply that they are inferior, or even superior to regular coating chocolate. I merely mean that they have been treated differently in their manufacture—perhaps they are one of the newer "Bloom-resistants" coatings, or have some ingredient added to inhibit streaking as much as possible. Whatever the reason, they will temper a little bit differently from ordinary coatings. That is why the directions are printed on their wrappers.

Chocolate must first be chopped into small lumps before it is melted. (It would be even better if you could grate it, but grating chocolate is at best a thankless job, and most persons would not care to take the time and trouble to do this. I don't, myself.) The easiest way to chop chocolate is with an ice pick on a board. Do not chop with the ice pick as you would if you were chopping ice. You push the pick down into the chocolate and a piece will snap off the big cake. Keep pushing the ice pick so that the pieces which snap off are not much larger than a walnut. The smaller the pieces are, the easier it will be to temper the chocolate, and the less chance you will take of overheating it. In this modern age, an *ice pick* may be very difficult to find. Unless you have an antique one around the house, a long, pointed awl from the local hardware store will serve as well. It will be a little harder to push into the chocolate because the point is not as tapering, or as sharp as that of an ice pick, but it will still do the job nicely.

Chop enough chocolate to fill the top of your double boiler two times since, as the lumps melt, the level will go down in the pot and you can add more. Put enough *hot* water in the bottom of the double boiler to come up around the sides of the top section when put in place. The water in the bottom section should not be over 140° or 150°F. After the chocolate has been over the hot water for a time, it will start melting around the sides of the pot. With a wooden spoon or flat smooth stick stir

The bulk chocolate is broken into small pieces on a board using an ice pick.

the lumps, trying to bring the bottom ones up to the top so that all the lumps come into contact with the hotter sides of the pot. As the water cools, you may turn on the flame under the double boiler, but *do not let the water boil* in the bottom section.

As the chocolate melts, keep adding a few more lumps until you have the top section filled with melted chocolate. It is a good idea to put in one lump of cocoa butter about the size of a walnut as you melt a potful of coating. The cocoa butter will thin the chocolate slightly, make it smoother to work and impart a nice satiny gloss to the finished candy.

After the chocolate has all melted, it should be stirred thoroughly and vigorously for several minutes. Stir carefully so that a lot of air is not incorporated in the coating. It should not be beaten—just stirred. Chocolate seems to have different densities within itself when it is just melted. At any rate, it is much smoother and more evenly textured if it has been stirred for a short time after melting.

The water in the bottom of the double boiler should now be tempered until it is not more than 125°F. This temperature will feel just nicely warm on your hand, but not so hot that you cannot tolerate immersing your hand in it. Allow the chocolate to remain over this water until you are ready to start dipping the chocolates, after which the coating must be tempered once more.

The final tempering is done on the marble slab just prior to the dipping process. You should have everything set out for the complete operation: the centers made from the fondant should be on sheets of waxed paper, which, in turn, are placed on sheets of corrugated cardboard, or pieces of thin plywood so they can be handled, the dipping paper is set beside the place where the chocolate will be used, also on a piece of plywood or stiff corrugated cardboard, and decoration, such as nuts, chocolate rice, dragées, etc. should be ready to hand.

With all preliminary preparations made, you may now pour the melted chocolate. When you lift the top out of the double boiler, wipe off the bottom of the part holding the chocolate so that no water will drip as you pour. *Make certain that the pot is dry* before carrying it to the marble and pouring, because *even a drop or two of water* in the chocolate will ruin it for dipping. Carefully pour a pool of chocolate on the marble.

Stir the melted chocolate vigorously several times to blend it well before using it.

If the dipping paper has been used previously, wipe it perfectly clean with a paper towel to remove any grease on the surface before reusing it.

Replace the partly empty top half in the double boiler, and, if you are going to do a lot of dipping, fill it up again with chopped chocolate so that can be melting while you dip.

We now come to a point which I could have brought up sooner, but this is as good a place to caution you as any. If your hands perspire, *you cannot dip chocolates* with them. The best way to find out is to sit holding hands with someone for several minutes. If you are married, the *safest* person to hold hands with is your wife or husband. If you are single, this is a good excuse to get chummy with your boy or girl friend. In any event, the person holding your hand should wear a rubber glove. This, because, even if *your* hands do not sweat, maybe *his* do and you would not be able to tell the difference. If, after a several-minute holding there is an appreciable amount of moisture on your hands, you will have to dip chocolates with a dipping fork. This is unfortunate, because it is much more cumbersome, un-handy and unprofessional, but it can be done. If your hands do not show moisture, you are ready to start.

DIRECTIONS FOR NON-PERSPIRING HANDS

When the pool of chocolate has been poured out on the slab for a minute or two, start mixing it around with the *fingertips only* of your right hand if you are right-handed, or your left hand if the reverse is true. You want to swirl the chocolate around, not enlarging the size of the puddle any more than is necessary, but enough to thoroughly agitate the chocolate and cool it. When first you touch it it will feel quite warm, even hot, to your fingers. As it is worked the temperature will start to lower.

The proper working temperature of coating chocolate is just below body temperature—about 85° to 90°F. This will feel slightly cool if you touch a spot of it to your wrist. As soon as the coating does feel cool to the touch, scrape it all together into as small a pile as possible, and you are ready to dip.

Hand dipping requires a skill that comes only with practice. The first time you dip Chocolate Creams you will probably make them pretty messy, but you will find that the skill will come fairly easily if you persevere. The fondant centers must

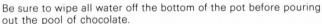

Be sure to wipe all water off the bottom of the pot before pouring out the pool of chocolate.

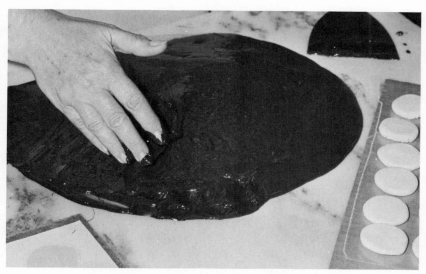

The poured-out chocolate is both cooled and mixed by pulling it in from the edges with the fingers of the dipping hand.

have a thin dried crust on them, and you should take all precautions against squashing them as they are coated with the chocolate. It is an excellent practice to turn over all the centers on the waxed paper before you start dipping to make certain that none of them will stick to the paper and break. Turning them also gives a little time for a crust to form on the bottom of each piece.

Pick up a center with your clean hand, carry it over and drop it into the chocolate pile. With the chocolate-covered fingers, pull a little of the chocolate over the piece; then, squeezing the chocolate off your fingers, pick the coated center out of the chocolate. Holding the center at about the first joints of your fingers, with the fingers very slightly opened, tap the back of your hand against the marble at the edge of the puddle of chocolate. This tapping is to knock the excess chocolate off the center. After tapping two or three times, close your fingers around the center, carry it over to the *farthest* corner of the dipping paper and slip it out of your fingers onto the paper, making sure that you slip it off with the bottom down. If you make certain that the bottom of the center is up in your fingers when you tap them, the candy will automatically fall right side up on the dipping paper when you turn your hand over to slip it off. As soon as the center is placed on the dipping paper, bunch your fingers together as tightly as possible, lift them slightly up off the center and wiggle them gently to lay a wiggled string of chocolate on the top of the Chocolate Cream. As you gain experience in dipping, you will be able to duplicate the shape of the wiggle on each center you dip, and to make differently shaped wiggles for differently flavored centers. This is called "stringing," and good stringing is a mark of a good professional dipper.

Each time you dip a center, deposit it on the dipping paper next to the previous one. Start always at the top, or far edge of the dipping paper; fill it with rows, working toward you to avoid drips and dragging strings of chocolate over the pieces already dipped. Make sure you do not place the chocolates so close together that they touch one another, and also make sure that your chocolate-covered fingers do not touch one piece as you are depositing another.

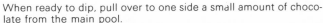

When ready to dip, pull over to one side a small amount of chocolate from the main pool.

Drop the center on the small pool of chocolate and turn it over, making certain all sides are covered.

If the pieces sag on the paper, with the chocolate in a thick ring around the bottom, you are not removing *enough* of the excess chocolate by tapping and squeezing before putting it on the dipping paper. If the center shows through the chocolate coating at any spot, you are removing *too much* of the coating as you put it on the dipping paper. You will soon learn how to gauge your dippings.

As the chocolate cools while you are dipping, you should add a little warm chocolate from the kettle. (Make sure you wipe the bottom of the kettle each time to avoid water drops.) The warm and cool chocolate must be thoroughly mixed with your dipping fingers, worked until the coating is cool enough to use.

When you have dipped all the centers, the chocolate remaining on the marble slab can be taken up with the fondant scraper and replaced in the double boiler for reuse. Do not cover the melted chocolate in the pot. Wait until it has completely cooled and solidified, or moisture will form on the underside of the lid and drip down into the chocolate.

Pick up the coated center and, at the side of the dipping pool, tap away surplus chocolate.

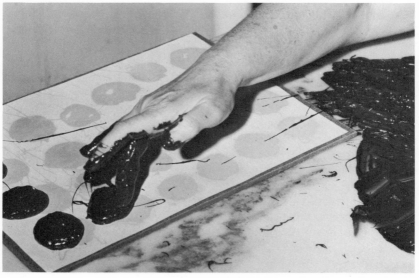

As you deposit it on the dipping paper, turn the candy over, then wiggle a string of chocolate on the top from a fingertip.

DIRECTIONS FOR THOSE WITH PERSPIRING HANDS

Up to the pouring out of the chocolate on the marble slab, the operations are exactly alike. Now, instead of swirling the chocolate around with the fingertips, you must work it and turn it over with the fondant scraper. Mix it well with this blade, testing a small drop on your wrist from time to time, until it is the correct temperature.

Use a dipping fork, which is very like a bonbon fork except it has two tines instead of a loop at the dipping end. The tines should be about the same size as the bonbon loop, and curved the same way. Lift a center with the fork. Drop it into the chocolate bottom side up and use the fork to pull a sheet of chocolate over it. Then lift the center with the fork and tap the hand on the marble to shake off the surplus coating. Do not rap your hand so hard on the marble slab that the center is forced down between the tines of the fork. This may easily happen, remember, because the center is soft fondant.

The Chocolate Cream is now carried over, turned upside down on the dipping paper and deposited on the bottom once more. The tines of the fork may be used for stringing the top of the candy in the same way as the finger method.

A Lot About Fondants

Perhaps the most important single process to learn in making fine candy is how to make fondant. This material, composed of sugar and water (or sugar, milk and butter), forms the basic material from which literally dozens of different kinds of candies are fashioned: chocolate creams, bonbons, peppermints and a host of other goodies.

There are two basic fondant recipes. Each is used for a specific kind of candy. They may be used for several different varieties of candies, all of which are important, and all of them are started in almost exactly the same way. They all require the use of a marble slab upon which the fondant is worked. The recipes are given in batch sizes for about six pounds per batch. This quantity of fondant is a useful one.

Since fondant keeps for many weeks (months, in fact), if it is covered and refrigerated, it is always a good idea to make up a couple of batches each time you cook. Two batches will fit into an ordinary mixing bowl which may then be covered with Saran Wrap or, alternatively, one of the tightly-covered plastic bowls which come equipped with a cover that snaps on around the edge. Either way, a clean kitchen towel, slightly moistened, should be packed flat onto the surface of the fondant after it has cooled, and the cover put in place on top of the towel. At intervals, if the stock fondant is to be stored for a long period, this towel should be removed and a fresh one substituted. The

The tools and ingredients needed for the center fondants are few and simple.

towels should be only *very slightly,* but evenly, damp. The purpose is only to prohibit the formation of a crystalline crust on the fondant. If this were to happen, the fondant, when worked up into chocolate creams, would "sugar out" and become hard and crunchy in their centers in a much shorter time than if the crust had not formed. Since no preservatives are added in the recipes given in this book, the shelf life of candies made from the fondants is shorter than that of commercial chocolate creams. In these, considerable quantities of preservatives are added to inhibit the hardening of the center fondant. Then, too, the fondant in 99% of all commercial creams is a water fondant, not a milk-and-butter fondant as presented here. A water-base fondant will remain soft for a longer time than a milk-and-butter fondant. The fondant used in commercial chocolate creams is, in fact, with a few modifications, the one used in this book as the Coating Fondant for bonbons only. This is not a rich fondant, but it has the property of accepting the addition of a "doctoring" ingredient in order to impart a high gloss to it when the finished bonbon has set and hardened.

Essentially, all the fondants are made in the same way.

They are cooked to the proper refinement temperature of the sugar, then worked on the marble slab until the sugar returns to a crystalline state. At this point the fondant is almost rock-hard. It is easily broken down, however, in the next stage—kneading the hard fondant for a few minutes until it assumes a semi-liquid condition. At this point it is placed in the storage container for ripening. After it has cooled in the container it is covered, as mentioned earlier, and put in the refrigerator. The fondant now returns to its hard stage, but not quite as hard as it was on the marble slab. It remains in this condition until it is to be made up into the individual candies.

Only two special tools are required in fondant making, be-sides, of course, the marble slab.

These are the candy thermometer and the fondant scrapers. The additional equipment list for fondant making is a large pan or kettle, a wooden spoon, measuring cups and spoons and the marble slab. You will also need two pot holders and a small bowl or a cup for chilled water. The water is used to condition the marble slab, not to test the cooking of the fondant. I might as well take the time right here to inform you that candymak-ing—if you intend to make *professional* candy, which is the entire purpose of this book—is an exact performance if candy is to be made with any degree of uniformity. To test a cooking batch of fondant to a "soft ball, or hard ball" stage by dropping a gob into a cup of water is, to my way of thinking, equivalent to the stone-age method of making fire by rubbing a stick of wood against the thigh bone of a saber-toothed tiger.

As with any kind of professional food preparation, candy should be cooked to an *exact* temperature. Cook the batch to *that* degree, and no other, and each batch of fondant is as uniform and predictable as it can be under those conditions. Allowances should be made in the degree figure to which the fondant is to be cooked, for the height above sea level where the candy is being made. (A chart, giving the temperature changes for this work at different altitudes is included in the Appendix.)

I have no intention of making you think that candymaking will become such a technical study that it will be bothersome or impossible to do in the home kitchen. Nothing is further from my mind. What I am attempting to do is to bring the making of really fine candy—better than you have ever had—

to your own home kitchen level. Take the exactness of fondant cooking for example. You put the ingredients on the fire to cook. Stir as directed in the individual recipes. Insert the candy thermometer into the fondant at a certain time, then cook the fondant until the temperature rises to a given point. At that point slide the pan off the fire. It is as simple as that, and, yet, it is as exact as that, since, if you cook each batch to the same thermometer degree, it follows that each batch will be uniform with all the other batches you make.

Compare this method with the "soft ball" test. How much water do you have in your testing cup? What is the temperature of that water? How much cooking fondant did you drop into the water? How long did you wait before you took the ball out and tested it between your fingertips for density? Who or what determines whether it is a soft ball, a medium-soft ball, a medium-hard ball or a stiff ball? You are dealing in this one test with five different variables, any one of which, at best, would be very difficult to duplicate each time candy was made. Have I made my point?

So, if you will realize that, throughout this book, we are dealing with tangibles—with definite degrees, quantities, measurements and times—that, when a recipe says cook to 236°F., it means *exactly* 236°F.—not 235½° or 236½°. If you get into the habit of working on the system outlined, you can, with a minimum of work, a minimum of fuss and a minimum of time, quite easily become the candy king or candy queen of your community!

Let us return to our discussion. The two fondants most used in making chocolate creams are: the Basic Center Fondant, and the Bonbon Coating Fondant. As I said earlier, most commercial candies are made with a water-sugar-corn syrup fondant. In this book we use a milk-sugar-butter fondant instead. The use of milk and butter makes an infinitely smoother center, one with a much richer flavor than that of the water fondant.

I will also repeat another statement made before. The recipes for fondants in this book are predicated on your having obtained a marble slab about 30 by 48 inches, and one inch thick. If you have a smaller slab, use half quantities of the fondant recipes. This halving applies only to the fondant recipes. All other candymaking can be done on the smaller slab with no alteration of quantities.

Here are the Center Fondant recipes called for throughout the book, unless otherwise stated. Note that they are called "recipes" not "formulas" since I have reduced them to kitchen-tested sizes and quantities from the professional formulas. PRELIMINARY PREPARATIONS: Before you begin a batch of candy, wash and wipe clean the marble slab and assemble all tools and ingredients. For fondants, a pan or kettle is needed— the smallest practical size is eight quarts and a ten-quart size is better, since fondant, expecially that made with milk, boils up quite alarmingly when it cooks. It will almost fill the kettle, and, indeed, will overflow the kettle if you stop stirring it for a time. A wooden spoon, a ¼-lb. stick of butter or margarine (unwrapped), cream of tartar (if required for the recipe used) measured out but left in the spoon, a small bowl of ice water and a fondant scraper (placed on one corner of the marble slab), two pot holders and a clean, damp sponge or lintless cloth. This about completes the preliminary preparations.

BASIC CENTER FONDANT

Granulated sugar: 5 lbs.　　　　　**Butter (or margarine): ¼-lb. stick**
Whole milk: 1 qt.　　　　　　　　**Cream of tartar*: ¼ tsp.**

Cook as directed and work up according to directions that follow.

---

*CREAM OF TARTAR is the chemical *potassium bitartrate* and, besides being used in fondant making, it is also an ingredient in baking powder; there are several medicinal uses, as well. The purpose of using cream of tartar in the fondant is to prevent the sugar from re-crystallizing when the fondant is worked up on the marble slab. Since cream of tartar is a bit "touchy" to use, most commercial candymakers substitute an alternate ingredient. Glucose (as it is called in the trade) performs the same action as cream of tartar and is somewhat easier to use. Corn syrup may be substituted for glucose, as I have done in the alternate Basic Center Fondant recipe on page 47.

Since we are dealing with small, controlled batches in this book, I have given a recipe using cream of tartar but have also included one using corn syrup. You may wish to try them both. You will find that fondants made with glucose will remain soft in the centers of finished chocolate creams for a little longer than will those made with cream of tartar. See footnote on glucose on page 47.

BASIC CENTER FONDANT (*Alternate Recipe*)

Granulated sugar: 5 lbs.
Whole milk: 1 qt.

Butter (or margarine): ¼-lb. stick
Karo light corn syrup (or
glucose*): 1 cup

This recipe will take a little longer to solidify on the marble slab and it will not get as hard as the other Basic Center Fondant. While it is of no great importance, you should be aware of the differences in the behavior of the ingredients. Cook as directed and work up according to directions that follow.

COOKING DIRECTIONS FOR BOTH BASIC FONDANTS

(A standard five-pound package of sugar may be used without weighing or measuring.) Put sugar in the kettle, add milk and corn syrup, if this is the recipe you are making. If you are using cream of tartar, this is added later. Stir with the wooden spoon until all the sugar is in suspension *before* putting kettle on the stove. Use a high flame or, if you are using electric heat, use the large burner set "high." As hot a temperature as possible under the kettle is needed. Add butter, and for the first few minutes, until the syrup begins to boil, stir only every minute or so. As soon as syrup begins a full, rolling boil, add cream of tartar (previously measured out and left in spoon for quick addition). Stir constantly from now on, in such a manner that the fondant is constantly in motion over the entire bottom of the kettle. The best pattern is a modified figure eight motion, starting with the spoon at the top of the kettle on the side away from you. Place the spoon down at the side, then pull it straight across the middle of the kettle until it touches the side near you. Holding it vertically all the while, push the spoon around the *right-hand side* of the kettle until it reaches the starting position across the kettle from you. Bring the spoon down across the middle of the kettle once more till it reaches your side, but this time push it back to the starting position around the *left-hand side* of the kettle. Repeat this motion, stirring slowly, just

*This recipe calls for the use of glucose in the original professional version but, because glucose may be difficult to obtain, especially in small quantities, I have substituted an almost universally obtainable home food product that will do as well: Karo light corn syrup, made by the Best Foods Division of Corn Products Company.

enough to keep the syrup moving. The faster it is stirred, the longer it will take the fondant to cook, because fast stirring exposes the surface to the air and tends to cool it somewhat, and reheating the syrup takes more time. As long as the syrup is moving around the bottom of the kettle, it will not scorch.

Listen to the *sound* of cooking: after the syrup has been boiling for a time the sound changes from the soft seething of the first rolling boil to a kind of sticky boiling sound. (It actually sounds *sticky,* and believe me, it is!) This will happen as the milk evaporates and the fluid becomes thicker. At this time the thermometer can be introduced into the boiling mass. Do not put a cold thermometer into hot syrup. Hold it over the boiling syrup a moment, then lower it until the end of the metal plate which supports the glass stem is immersed. Hold it there for another moment, then the thermometer can slowly be lowered into the syrup, sliding the retaining clip on the thermometer over the side of the kettle as you do so.

The temperature will shoot up rapidly, stopping somewhere around 220°F. The syrup will remain at this temperature for several minutes, then the level slowly starts to rise again. Con-

To get accurate readings of the thermometer, get your eyes on a level with the mercury column.

tinue stirring, but avoid hitting the glass column of the thermometer with the spoon; also avoid knocking the thermometer
about on the side of the kettle. Make sure that the thermometer
is deeply placed in the syrup, not just under the surface. As soon
as the temperature registers 236°F. slide the kettle off the
flame, and *then* turn the heat off. This is especially important
if you are using an electric range, since the burner retains its
heat well after the switch is turned off, and cooking will continue past the desired temperature level.

(NOTE: All temperatures given are for sea level. Adjust for
higher altitudes according to directions on page 173. If you
wish, it may be a good idea for you to replace *all* temperatures
in the recipes, writing them in, before you begin to cook, so as
to avoid slip-ups and overcooking.)

As soon as you have the kettle off the stove, remove the
thermometer and the spoon from the kettle and place them
where they can safely drip and cool. Dip your fingers in the cup
of ice water you have previously placed on the marble slab and
sprinkle drops of water all over the slab. Put the bowl well out
of the way and, with the damp sponge you have previously
made ready, wipe away all the crystals from one side of the
kettle right down to the surface of the hot fondant. *Be careful!*
Do not let your finger or hand *touch* the hot fondant or you will
leave that portion of your skin on the surface of the candy. Be
sure to wipe off a *wide enough area* to allow you to pour out
without *any* crystals touching the fondant.

Take the pot holders and carry the kettle to the marble slab,
being careful not to swirl the fondant about as you walk. Pour
the fondant on the slab of wet marble, beginning at one side and
walking along with the kettle, rather than reaching out to pour.
As the last of the fondant is poured you must quickly upend the
kettle (away from you) so that it makes a complete somersault,
rotating until it is upright again. The purpose of this is to cut
off the drip from the side and also to keep any crystals from
falling off the inside of the kettle and onto the fondant.

Now is the time to dispose of the kettle, putting it in the sink
and filling it with *hot* water. When filled, put the thermometer
and the wooden spoon in it to soak, and by the time the fondant
is worked up, all that will be needed is to rinse off the imple-
ments and the kettle. This is a good routine to establish because

The marble slab should be sprinkled with ice-cold water just before pouring out the hot fondant.

first, the thermometer stands less chance of being broken if it is soaked clean immediately; second, should you be wanting to make a second batch right away you are saved a half-hour's cleaning time; third, establishing a routine becomes easier each time the routine is followed until it is habitual, and everything is done the same way every time.

When two or three minutes have elapsed, tap the fondant with your fingertip *very quickly*. If you *press* your fingertip into it, you will be burned, but a quick tap will make a dent in the surface without the fondant sticking to your finger. Watch the dent. If it levels immediately, wait another minute or two. If the dent remains hollow, filling in very slowly, it is ready for you to begin to work.

WORKING THE FONDANT: The first time you work a batch of fondant will be rather exciting. First of all, you will find that the fondant will want to do what *it* wants to, not what you want it to do. Your job will be to keep it moving, once you start to work it, keeping it in as neat a mass as you can, as near to the center of the slab as possible. Aim to do this *without stopping, once you start*—and without throwing the sticky mess on the

Always pour with the top of the kettle facing away from you.

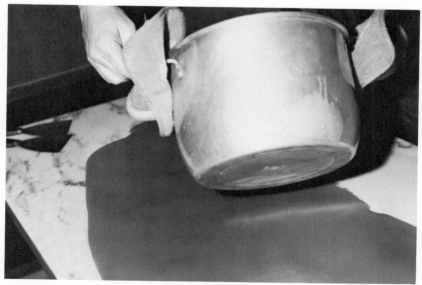

As the last of the syrup is poured out, give the kettle a complete
turn to cut off the drip.

Start to work the fondant by scraping the knife along and up the right side of the pool.

floor, the walls, yourself or the ceiling! There is little exaggeration in that statement, for probably you will be rather sticky and gooey after your first fondant working. But do not let that daunt you. Keep in mind that you are the one directing this operation, not the fondant.

The second trial will go much more easily and after three or four times, you will work up a batch of fondant with the best of us. Work the fondant with the fondant scraper—that putty-knife-like blade, remember? With the very first stroke you will see why I told you to make certain that the blade runs clear through the handle. At the beginning, the fondant will be so sticky that it may pull the knife right out of your hand if you are not careful. Hold the scraper so that your fingers are up and the back of your hand is down toward the marble. Take your first stroke around the right-hand side of the poured-out fondant, making the stroke with the front edge of the blade flat on the surface of the marble. Keep pressing the blade tightly down on the marble, for it will have a tendency to ride up on top of the fondant if insufficient downward pressure is exercised. As you push the knife away from you, cut into the fondant about

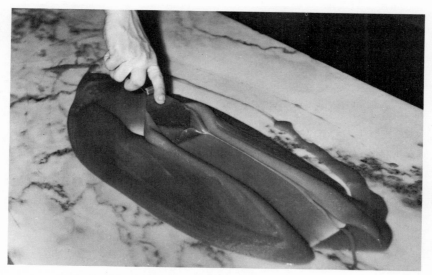

At the far side of the pool, turn the blade and pull it down through the middle of the fondant.

half of the width of the blade. Continue the forward stroke around the right side of the fondant, curving it in at the far end until you arrive at the middle, opposite you.

Then, turning your wrist and the scraper, pull it back toward you through the middle, mashing down with all your strength to squeeze the fondant out from both sides of the blade. Without hestitating, make another forward stroke, this time around the *left* side of the fondant on the marble. Return through the middle, turning the scraper and squashing the fondant down, as before. Continue in this manner, alternating your strokes and working through the fondant. When you/start, the fondant will be translucent, slightly yellow in color; it will remain so and also stay sticky for several minutes as you work it; then suddenly you will see that the fondant is turning whiter. When this change of color occurs, you will also note that the mass seems to be less sticky than it was at the start.

NOW is the time to speed up your strokes as much as possible, and this is a very critical time for the fondant. You must not miss any strokes, nor allow the fondant to remain motionless, because if you do, it will re-crystallize into grainy sugar

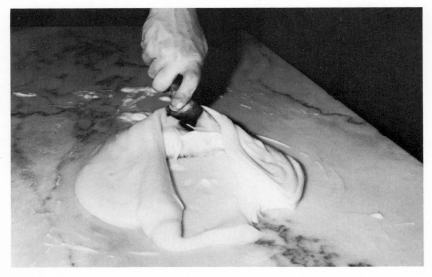

After being worked for a time, the fondant will turn milky-white and feel less sticky. Keep working it without stopping.

once again. You *must* continue without stopping, and the fondant will become more soft, more white, until before your very eyes it will suddenly turn into a solid mass! Whatever position your hand and the scraper were in at that moment, they will become locked in the fondant, like Excalibur locked inside the stone! The scraper will be about as hard to remove from the fondant as Excalibur was, too, and you may justly feel as exuberant as did King Arthur, when he succeeded in removing the sword.

Take a few minutes to catch your breath, and, while doing so, scrape all the drips and splashes from around the marble slab. These may either be scraped up and discarded, or they can be worked as a miniature batch until they, too, harden up, at which time they can be added to the main batch. As you gain dexterity in working fondant you will find that your drips and splashes are fewer and fewer.

If the handle of your scraper has become covered with sticky fondant, as it almost certainly will on your first batch, you may take the time to clean it and your hands. Now place the bowl or container in which the fondant will be stored for ripening in

Suddenly the fondant will harden into a rock-like mass.

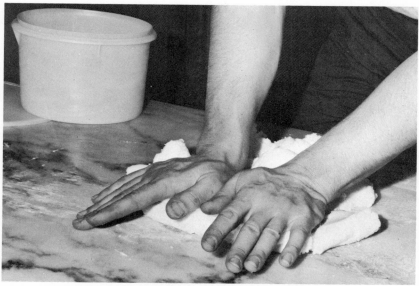

The hard mass must now be broken down until it is once again soft and free from lumps. Knead it like bread dough.

a handy spot, and start to break down the structure of the hard fondant. Do this with the heels of your hands, exactly as if you were kneading bread. However, since some of my readers may not have made bread, I will explain the process in detail. Place both hands over the hard fondant, with the heels of the hands against the side of the lump facing you. Push against the lump until it breaks away, then squash it down and away from you, rubbing it against the marble slab.

Pull the fondant back into a lump and repeat the squashing action. You may find it necessary to lift the fondant from the marble with the scraper, in order to pile it back into a lump for kneading. You continue this kneading, rubbing the fondant hard against the marble to squeeze out any small lumps. You will feel these lumps under your hands as you work. After kneading the mass for a minute or two, it will quickly revert to a semi-liquid state. Continue to knead only until you can feel no more lumps within the mass, then, with the scraper pull the mass together into a lump and lift it up in your hands. Pat it quickly into a ball—(it will be quite runny at this stage)—and drop the ball into the storage container. (The reason for balling it before putting it into the container is that there is less chance this way for air to become trapped between the fondant and the walls of the container.) Jiggle the container and the fondant will settle and level. Put aside until it cools, first placing the damp towel on the surface to prevent the fondant from drying out. Do not seal the container until the fondant has cooled completely, or it will sweat and dissolve. After cooling—a matter of at least two or three hours—cover the container and refrigerate until time to use it. Do not allow the fondant to freeze.

Fondant should ripen for at least two days before being made up into any of the individual kinds of creams described in the separate recipes. However, here I will tell you the action of the fondant when used. For making any given flavor of chocolate cream, cut out of the storage container a portion of the ripened fondant large enough to make as many pieces as you desire. It will once again be hard, although not as hard as when it hardened on the slab during working. This portion is placed on the marble and any desired flavoring and food color is added to it. You may use either liquid or paste food colors, but paste color is superior to liquid. Work the coloring and flavoring into the fondant with the scraper, kneading it into a smooth paste. Use very little color at one time. It is very easy to add more color, but if you add too much to start, the only way you can lighten the color of the fondant is to add more raw fondant. You might end up making twice as much of one kind as you intended. The color and flavor should be thoroughly worked into the fondant. No streaks of color should show. If the fondant becomes so soft that it is unmanageable, it may be thickened by the addition of xxxx powdered sugar. Never add more than one teaspoonful of sugar to a batch of fondant the size of your double fists or the xxxx sugar will start a crystallizing process that will make the fondant turn gritty and grainy. A center of a chocolate cream made with fondant should be silky-smooth as you eat it. Against the roof of your mouth you should feel not the slightest bit of graininess.

Almost fifty years ago, as a small boy, one of my very favorite confections was a confection known then as Opera Cream. The particular candy store which sold this carried it in two flavors: vanilla and chocolate. Inside the candy case were two shallow pans filled with the cream which was marked off into squares, perhaps an inch in size. Two squares of the cream were sold for a penny, and the owner would slide the squares off the pan with a small spatula. The Opera Cream was soft and he slipped the squares from the spatula to a small piece of waxed paper, from which the candy could be eaten. It was smooth, rich-tasting and delightful. It was not for several years, until I was helping my mother make candy, that I learned that Opera Cream was really the fondant I have just told you how to make, flavored with vanilla or chocolate and spread about ½ inch thick in pans. Perhaps his formula was a bit different, but it was a milk-sugar-butter fondant, nonetheless.

COATING FONDANT

The next most important fondant used in candymaking is the one used for coating bonbons. Bonbons are a confection better known in Europe than in this country, although some of the better confectionery stores here sell bonbons. In France the name for *any* candy is bonbon, pronounced something like "bone-bone" but in England and in America the name bonbon applies to that particular kind of candy that has a fondant center, which may be plain or may contain fruits or nuts, and is coated with another type of fondant that hardens to a gloss retaining the moisture in the center fondant.

Bonbon coating fondant is a different kind than that we have just made. It does not contain either cream of tartar or light corn syrup to inhibit crystallization. In place of these agents, bonbon fondant uses what is known to the professional candymakers as "bonbon doctor," a mixture of liquids, the recipe for which follows:

BONBON DOCTOR

8% acetic acid: 1 oz.   Pure grain alcohol: 1 oz.
Glycerine: 1¼ ozs.   Karo light corn syrup: ½ oz.

Any drug store can make up the solution for you, but if you have that done, omit the Karo light corn syrup from the formula, and add that yourself. Some states sell grain alcohol or permit it to be sold. Usually liquor stores in those states handle the product. New York State prohibits the sale of grain alcohol, and you may even have to get a prescription from your doctor to have the formula made up, unless you are friendly with your druggist and explain to him what the material is to be used for.

For that matter you can even make up the solution yourself, if the druggist is reluctant to do so. Any photographic supply store will have glacial acetic acid. For the purposes of this recipe we can call glacial acetic acid "100% strength." One teaspoonful of this acid and 11½ teaspoonfuls of water will approximate 8% acetic acid nearly enough for our doctoring solution.

(Your only difficulty would lie in finding grain alcohol. Glycerine can be purchased in drug stores in small quantities.) If your photographic store is out of glacial acetic acid, they are certain to have 28% acetic acid. This may also be used, and with this strength, one teaspoonful of glacial acetic acid should be mixed with four teaspoonfuls of water, since 28% acetic acid is roughly only one-quarter the strength of the glacial.

BONBON COATING FONDANT

Sugar: 5 lbs.
Water: 3 cups

Knox flavorless gelatin: 1
   envelope
Bonbon doctor: 4 tsps.

Put gelatin in ½ cup of cold water, stirring until it is dissolved. Add the bonbon doctor, stir and strain into a clean cup. Put the sugar and remaining water into a *large* kettle (not less than 8- to 10-quart capacity.) Place on the stove over a high flame; stir until sugar is dissolved, when no more stirring is necessary. Put candy thermometer in candy and attach to kettle. Cook to 245°F. Then add gelatin-doctor solution very quickly.

The fondant will boil up violently, and you should stir the boiling candy rapidly, watching the thermometer closely all the time. Cook to 236°F., then remove kettle from the fire immediately. (It will take only a minute or two for the temperature to rise to this level after adding gelatin mixture.) Remove the thermometer from the kettle, and continue to stir for a few minutes until the foam settles and disappears.

Sprinkle the marble with ice water (p. 49) then pour the fondant out on it; allow to cool, then work as described for the first fondant recipe (p. 50). This one will take just a little longer to work than the cream fondant. Break down with the hands and put into a covered container for storage with moist towel over it. When this fondant is broken down it becomes a very soft, runny, sticky mass that settles easily in the container.

An alternate recipe for a fondant good for coating bonbons uses cream of tartar.

ALTERNATE COATING FONDANT

Sugar: 5 lbs.
Water: 1 qt.

Cream of tartar: ¼ tsp.

Stir the sugar and water in a large kettle until the sugar is in suspension, then place over a high flame. Continue stirring until the sugar is all dissolved. At the moment of full boil, add the cream of tartar, stir it in completely, and cook to 236°F.; remove the kettle from the fire. Wipe down the crystals on one side of the kettle and pour out on the sprinkled marble slab (p. 49). When cool, work as for other fondants with fondant scraper, break down and place in container to store.

The difference between this recipe and the one preceding is mainly a matter of density. This alternate recipe, containing cream of tartar, makes a harder coating than the one using the doctor. However, the gloss is not as high, which may be objectionable to some candymakers. Also, the cream of tartar recipe crusts very rapidly when remelted, making constant stirring almost a necessity while the bonbons are being dipped. This stirring is not too big a chore, however, because normally you would stir the fondant each time you dropped in a piece of center for coating.

Hard Crack — and How to Use It

Next in importance to fondant, in candymaking, is "hard crack." This is a candy which has been cooked to an extremely high degree, so high in fact, that the sugar crystallizes into a hard, clear mass. It contains very little water, most having been evaporated during the cooking process. It is usually crystal clear, but, when pulled, as for taffy or stick candy, it incorporates considerable air in the form of tiny bubbles that impart an opaqueness to the candy.

Hard crack is the name given to this form of sugar cookery, simply because it graphically describes the physical properties of the candy. It *is* hard, and it *does* crack when struck or dropped, very much like glass. It is the base from which is made many different kinds of candies. The hard candies so familiar around the Christmas holidays are made out of hard crack. Lollipops, of course, come from the same material. Candy canes, peanut brittle, sourballs—all are hard-crack candies.

Hard crack is so easy to cook that even a child can make lollipops with very little trouble. About the only thing they would have to watch out for is not to splatter themselves with the super-hot syrup, which would instantly burn the skin wherever it landed. Hard crack is cooked to the highest temperatures of any of the many kinds of candy and, usually, only professional candy thermometers have a scale that goes high enough to encompass the *entire* range of hard-crack cookery.

An assortment of both patty lollipops and molded lollipops, showing some potentials.

Because of the ease with which hard crack can be made, I am going to start your candymaking career off with some recipes for lollipops and brittles. Lollipops are made either in fancy molds or as round patties formed directly on the surface of the marble slab. The molds are available from confectioners' supply houses, and usually have three or more cavities so that that many pops can be made simultaneously. Used molds are sometimes available, and these are much cheaper than the new ones. Since the molds cost a few dollars each, unless you have a moppet or two in the family or intend to make a lot of this kind of candy, perhaps you might just as well confine your lollipops to the patty kind.

Whatever style you choose, you will need a supply of lollipop sticks. These are also sold in confectioners' supply houses, and some large bakery supply stores might also carry them. In a pinch, you can purchase ⅛-inch by three-foot dowels from the hardware store and cut them into six-inch lengths. You can also find small-diameter dowels in hobby stores that sell model-maker's wood in different sizes. Do *not* buy balsawood sticks for lollipops, because balsawood is entirely lacking in tensile or shear strength, and will break the moment you try to eat the lollipop. Hard crack as used for making lollipops is very simple.

BASIC HARD CRACK

Sugar: 2 cups
Water: 1 cup

Karo light corn syrup: 1 cup
Lollipop sticks

All the ingredients are placed together in the kettle and stirred until the sugar is completely in suspension. Put the kettle on a high flame and continue stirring mixture until the sugar is all dissolved, then stop stirring. Put the thermometer in the kettle as soon as you stop the stirring, and cook the candy to 300°F. At about 260°F., paste colors may be added. (See p. 57.) Remove from the burner at 300°F. and as soon as the seething has settled, add the desired flavor and stir it in quickly. Wipe down the crystals from the sides of the kettle (p. 49), then pour the candy in small round patties on the slab, covering the ends of the lollipop sticks laid out previously.

Some of the flavors used in hard crack are slightly different from those used in fondant. Most are essential oils that are *very* strong and *very* potent. Some others are synthetic flavors. Make sure all of these are designated for use in hard crack. Some fondant flavors are synthetic, too, but their chemical structure is different, and, if used at the very high temperatures of lollipop material, they would boil out, leaving the candy flavorless, or they would change chemically, imparting an entirely—and not always pleasant—new flavor.

You might also find that some of the colors you use will change in the hot candy. Red is one color that may turn brownish when it hits the molten mass of sugar. It also takes more color to tint a batch of hard crack than it does to color a batch of fondant the same size. This is because it is harder to affect the transparent candy and color it than it is to color a batch of opaque white fondant.

While the candy is cooking, you can prepare the marble slab for receiving the lollipops (the method is different from others). The marble should be clean, of course, then oiled with a very thin layer of mineral oil—the same mineral oil you buy in the drug store for use as a laxative. In years past, before the medicinal qualities of mineral oil were well known, it was sold in bakery and confectioners' supply houses under the name of "slab oil" for about a dollar a gallon. Now it is difficult to find as slab oil, but many shops besides drug stores sell it as mineral oil, although at a considerably higher price.

A small puddle is poured out and rubbed all over the marble slab with the palm of the hand. It is thick, so rub it hard to spread it out well. Only a very thin layer of oil is necessary to prepare the slab.

Now lay out a row of lollipop sticks, or as many rows as the marble will accommodate, and arrange them so that there is room to pour a patty of hard crack over one end of each stick without touching the other sticks. By staggering the sticks, allowing the ends of every other one to stick out about 2 or 2½ inches from the ones in between, you can place many more sticks in a row. Here are some recipes for making lollipops.

ORANGE LOLLIPOPS

Sugar: 2 cups
Water: 1 cup
Karo light corn syrup: 1 cup
Orange food coloring

Powdered citric acid (optional):
1 tsp. (See p. 65, note)
Oil of orange: 1 tsp.

Place the sugar, water and corn syrup in a medium-sized saucepan and stir all together until the sugar is in suspension. Place over high heat and stir until the sugar is completely melted. Now cook to 260°F., then add enough food coloring to color the batch a nice deep orange. Continue to cook to 300°F., then remove the pan from the heat. With a damp sponge or a cloth wrapped around the handle of the wooden spoon, wipe all the crystals from the inside of the pan above the liquid, and then add citric acid (if used) and half-teaspoon oil of orange. The syrup will "boil up" in the pan when you add these ingredients, so be ready to stir rapidly with the wooden spoon to mix them in and reduce the bubbles. As soon as the bubbling has stopped, add the remaining half-teaspoon oil of orange and stir in well.

Pour out patties over the ends of each lollipop stick. The

patties should be not much larger than two inches in diameter. If there is excess syrup when all of the sticks have a patty poured on them, pour remainder out on the slab to make a large cake. When hard, this can be broken up into small pieces and eaten.

Within a minute or two after pouring, the lollipops will be hard and you can *slip* them off the marble slab. Wrap the candy end in a square of waxed paper, and they are finished. Do not attempt to grasp the sticks and *lift* the lollipop up, or you will probably break the stick off where it enters the candy. The suction is quite strong on the slab, due to the sealing effect of the mineral oil. But they will slide off easily, and, once they start sliding, may even lift up easily. *Makes about 50 lollipops.*

NOTE: Several batches of lollipops can be made without having to add mineral oil to the marble. Merely respread the oil with the palm of the hand after each batch is removed.

LEMON LOLLIPOPS

Sugar: 2 cups
Water: 1 cup
Karo light corn syrup: 1 cup
Oil of lemon: 1 tsp.

Yellow food coloring
Powdered citric acid (optional):
1 tsp.

Follow procedures, as for Orange Lollipops, dividing flavoring and adding it in two equal portions. *Makes about 50 lollipops.*

LIME LOLLIPOPS

Sugar: 2 cups
Water: 1 cup
Karo light corn syrup: 1 cup
Oil of lime: 1 tsp.

Green food coloring
Powdered citric acid (optional):
1 tsp.

Follow procedures, as for Orange Lollipops, dividing flavoring and adding it in two equal portions. *Makes about 50 lollipops.*

NOTE: All three flavors of lollipops may be made without adding citric acid if a sweeter candy is desired, in which case the flavoring should be reduced to ¾ teaspoon, divided into equal parts and added as directed. The citric acid imparts a more bitter, or sour, taste to orange, lemon or lime flavors that is pleasing to many.

PEPPERMINT LOLLIPOPS

Sugar: 2 cups
Water: 1 cup

Karo light corn syrup: 1 cup
Oil of peppermint: ½ tsp.

Follow procedures, as for Orange Lollipops, to point of removing kettle from the heat. After it has been removed, wait a minute or two until the bubbling stops, then stir in the flavoring. (Keep your face averted as you pour in the peppermint, as the steam arising is intense and powerful, and the mint fumes will cause the eyes to water profusely.) Pour out, as soon as flavoring is well mixed, on the previously laid sticks. *Makes about 50 lollipops.*

A WORD ABOUT WINTERGREEN FLAVORING

First, a word about the flavoring used in making wintergreen candy. In times past the flavor was true oil of wintergreen. This was an expensive flavoring, even then, and, in a couple of decades, oil of sweet birch was used in place of the true oil of wintergreen, and was called either synthetic oil of wintergreen, or by its own name, oil of sweet birch. As time passed, oil of sweet birch also became so expensive that few confectioners were willing to use it in their factories, so a real synthetic was devised, called *methyl salicylate.* This was then sold as either *methyl salicylate,* or synthetic oil of wintergreen.

I might also take the time here to explain that a *synthetic* flavoring is still a very good one. The word synthetic implies that the product is exactly the same as the natural one it is supplanting, except that it was achieved in a laboratory instead of by nature. It is the *imitation* flavors that are not as good as the real thing. Imitation means that it is made in a laboratory to approach the real flavor, as nearly as they can. It is not implied that an imitation flavor tastes exactly the same as a true flavor; most of the time they do not. The quality also varies from one manufacturer to another. Usually, an imitation flavor *tastes* like the true flavor *smells.* Since our taste mechanism and our sense of smell are very closely related and, in fact, operate together, the imitation flavors come near enough to be used in foods.

WINTERGREEN LOLLIPOPS

Sugar: 2 cups
Water: 1 cup

Karo light corn syrup: 1 cup
Oil of sweet birch: 1 Tbsp.

Follow procedures, as for Orange Lollipops, dividing flavoring and adding it in two equal portions. If either of the substitute flavorings described in the preceding paragraph are used, the same quantity (1 tablespoonful) will be right. *Makes about 50 lollipops.*

A WORD ABOUT CINNAMON FLAVORING

Oil of cassia is an oil extracted from the bark of the cassia tree, or the cinnamon tree as it is sometimes called. Actually, cinnamon bark as you buy it in food stores, either in stick form or as a finely ground powder, is made from sucker shoots of the true cinnamon tree, while the oil of cassia used as cinnamon flavoring is extracted from the cassia tree. Both trees belong to the same genus, and the flavor of both is alike, but oil of cassia is like dynamite. It is so strong that it may burn your skin if you get a drop on a tender spot. Therefore, be careful when you add it to the hot syrup, to protect your face and eyes from the highly irritating fumes.

CINNAMON LOLLIPOPS

Sugar: 2 cups
Water: 1 cup
Karo light corn syrup: 1 cup

Red food coloring
Oil of cassia: ⅛ tsp.

Follow procedures, as for Orange Lollipops, except for adding the oil of cassia. After coloring matter is added, then the oil of cassia (note precaution in paragraph on p. 67) and stir until it and the color are well mixed into the syrup. *Makes about 50 lollipops.*

All of these lollipop recipes will make about 50 patty lollipops or about a dozen lollipops cast in metal molds. If you have some of the clear toy molds used to make fancy lollipops, they should be cleaned, then carefully coated inside with mineral oil. Make sure that the oil covers all the deep places in the mold. After oiling the mold, tie it together with a piece of twine, making sure that the twine does not pass over any of the filling holes in the mold. Pour the syrup into the mold quickly, filling all the cavities, then push lollipop sticks down into the candy and hold them for a second or two to make sure they will stand up straight. Watch the molds while you are working and if any of the sticks sag, straighten them until the candy hardens enough to support them. Molded lollipops take a lot longer to harden than do patty pops. This is because the mold retains heat when the syrup is poured into it, keeping the syrup hot for a longer time, and also because there is a greater quantity of syrup in a molded lollipop than in a patty lollipop; finally, the marble slab chills the syrup as soon as it is poured out for patties. Wait until you are sure that the syrup has hardened before cutting the string and opening the mold, and then allow the lollipop to cool completely before wrapping it in the waxed paper.

BRITTLES

Now that you have tried your hand at making the easiest kind of candy, we can advance a little and make some of the more complicated recipes for brittles. These are still made out of hard crack or, rather, the candy is cooked to the hard-crack stage. We have a choice of several kinds of brittles. Let's start with peanut brittle. The recipe I have here is the best one I have ever discovered for peanut brittle, and it is almost as easy to make as lollipops.

Usually, in homemade peanut brittle, the candy is so thick and so tough that it is very hard to eat. Even some commercial peanut brittles are thick and hard. Peanut brittle should be what its name implies: brittle, not tough. Brittle may mean that the material is *hard*, but it *is* brittle—it breaks easily, or fractures when it is eaten.

Two conditions will make peanut brittle a true brittle: the incorporation of air into the hard crack, and pulling of the candy out into a thin sheet that supports the peanuts within it. We achieve both these conditions with our brittle recipe.

While any kind of peanuts may be used in peanut brittle, by far the tastiest ones are the little round Spanish peanuts. These should be purchased raw—not roasted. They are sold by bakery and confectioners' supply houses, raw, shelled, with the hulls still on. You may have to order them, since these nuts are often not a regular stock item. Also, some bigger houses may require you to buy them in ten-pound quantities, especially if they have to order them specially. This need not worry you. First, the raw nuts will keep for a long, long time, if stored in a tightly sealed container, or for a year or more if stored in a sealed plastic bag in a freezer. However, the first batch of this peanut brittle will be your downfall, and you will be making it frequently because it is so delicious that you will never get enough of it. If you are one of the few persons who do not like peanut brittle, do not let this deter you from making a sample batch. I can almost guarantee that if you may not have liked peanut brittle up to the moment you sampled this one, you will be converted to an ardent lover of the candy with your first bite!

Peanut brittle is made right on the marble slab treated with mineral oil (p. 63), as were the lollipops. However, you must have a pair of tough, thick gloves to make this candy. A pair of hard-crack pulling-gloves may be purchased at a confectioners' supply house, or you can substitute a pair of leather-palmed work gloves with success if you are careful in using them. Work gloves are sold in hardware stores and other shops, with or without cuffs on them. Get a pair without cuffs if possible. The palms and fingers *must* have the leather right down to the tips of the fingers. The backs may be made of fabric. *Do not* get the gloves made of smooth top-surface leather. The kind you must use are made out of gray split leather that looks like a very coarse suede. This kind of leather will not stick to the peanut brittle while you are working it. In order to prepare the gloves for use, a little mineral oil should be thoroughly rubbed into the leather. Do not saturate the gloves with the oil; just apply a small amount and work it into the finger parts, especially around the tips. The palms need not be oiled, since, if you work properly, you will not have the candy touch the palm parts of the gloves.

The gloves are used to pull out the sheet of candy to paper thinness, one of the ways to make it tender. The incorporation of air into the hard crack is done chemically, by the addition of baking soda to the hot syrup before pouring it out on the marble slab. One of the secrets of the wonderful flavor in this peanut brittle is the use of the raw peanuts that are cooked in the candy as you make it. The flavor of the nuts permeates the hard crack, the hulls color it slightly and also add some flavor. The hard crack for peanut brittle *need not be stirred while cooking* until after you set it back by the addition of the cold peanuts. However, after the peanuts are in the syrup you should stir occasionally to make sure the nuts are immersed in the syrup to cook, and also to prevent any nuts from resting on the bottom of the pan and burning. After the temperature starts to rise at the end of the cooking, you must stir to prevent the syrup from scorching. A very light scorching is permissable and gives, in fact, a better flavor to the brittle as well as a good color. Do not let the candy scorch to the point where it turns dark brown, though, or it will have a burned taste that is somewhat unpleasant. Here is my recipe for peanut brittle:

PEANUT BRITTLE

Sugar: 2 cups
Water: 1 cup
Karo light corn syrup: 1 cup
Raw Spanish peanuts: 2 cups

Butter or margarine: 1 Tbsp.
Salt: ¼ tsp.
Baking soda: ¼ tsp.

Combine the sugar, water and Karo light corn syrup in a large kettle and stir with a wooden spoon until the sugar is well suspended. Place over high heat and stir until the sugar is melted, then cook without stirring to 236°F. At this point add peanuts and salt; stir until nuts are well mixed with the syrup.

Continue to cook, stirring once every few minutes until the thermometer reaches 295°F. Stir more frequently toward the end, as the syrup may begin to scorch. At 295°F. remove from the heat and add the butter, stirring it into the syrup until it is completely melted, then add the baking soda. The syrup will froth up alarmingly in the kettle as you start to stir in the baking soda. Mix it well, and pour the brittle out on the oiled marble slab while it is still frothing. Scrape all of the nuts out of the kettle, and onto the brittle. Then spread out the brittle as thinly as you can with the wooden spoon. You must work as fast as you can, because the chilled slab will cool the brittle very rapidly.

As soon as you can, after spreading the brittle, loosen it from the slab with a long spatula, a long steel knife or a fondant scraper and, putting on the oiled leather gloves, lift the brittle with the scraper and one hand and quickly flop it over on its other side.

Immediately start to pull out the brittle sheet as thinly as possible. Work rapidly, grasping the brittle with the gloves and pulling on all sides. Do not hold the brittle for a long time or the gloves will sink into the hot candy and become stuck there. Also, if you maintain a hold on the brittle for more than an instant, the heat will transfer through the gloves and you may blister your hands.

Reach well into the middle of the sheet to pull there, too, not pulling just around the edges. The brittle can be pulled out so thin that the peanuts are little lumps in a thin sheet. Perhaps the first batch you make will be thick in places, and unevenly pulled. This is to be expected, since you will not know how the material feels or works. With a little practice, however, you will be able to pour a batch, flop it over and pull it out into a sheet in minutes.

Within five minutes after it is pulled the brittle will be completely hard and ready to break up into smaller pieces. This is done with the fondant scraper, holding a large piece of brittle in one hand and tapping it with the edge of the scraper. Wait until the brittle is completely cold before packing it for storage in a wide-mouthed jar with a tightly fitting cover. I promise you it will not be stored for very long, but will be eaten with relish.

PECAN BRITTLE

Sugar: 2 cups
Water: 1 cup
Karo light corn syrup: 1 cup
Shelled pecans, pieces: 3 cups

Butter or margarine: 1 Tbsp.
Salt: ¼ tsp.
Baking soda: ¼ tsp.

Cook the sugar, water and corn syrup over high heat to 300°F., stirring with a wooden spoon only until the sugar is completely dissolved. Remove from the burner and add the pecans and salt, stirring them in thoroughly. Add the butter while stirring. Add the baking soda, stirring rapidly while the candy is frothing. Pour out on the lightly oiled slab while it is still a bit frothy. Spread out as much as possible with the back of the wooden spoon; then, donning oiled leather gloves, lift the sheet with the fondant scraper and flop it over. Pull the candy out into a thin sheet, not quite as thin as called for in the peanut brittle recipe. Allow to cool completely, then break into small pieces with the fondant scraper and store in a tightly sealed jar.

Variation: WALNUT BRITTLE. This is made exactly the same as pecan brittle, except that 3 cups of shelled English walnuts are substituted for the pecans. If the walnuts are in large pieces, break them smaller with the fingers. *Do not chop them or grind them.*

An excellent nut brittle may be made by combining half pecans and half English walnuts. Nut brittles may be made with almost any kind of nuts; for instance, pistachio nuts or filberts. The filberts should be cut into three or four pieces before using. You will note that in all the nut brittles except peanut brittle, the hard crack is cooked to the final temperature *before* adding the nuts. This is because the other nuts can be eaten raw, but peanuts are not palatable in the raw state.

If you like to have the nut flavor imparted to the hard crack, you could put the nuts in before the cooking is finished, but not as soon as for the peanuts, because that would overcook the other nuts and they would lose flavor and texture. The nuts could be added to the hard crack at around 280°F. You might experiment, making the first batch as the recipes state, then adding the nuts earlier for the second batch. You can then choose your favorite.

We now come to a recipe for a candy that I have named Royal Brittle, though it really is not so much a brittle as a block candy. This is made in a different way from most other hard-crack candy.

ROYAL BRITTLE

Shelled walnuts: 1 cup
Shelled pecans: 1 cup
Candied cherries: 1½ cups
Candied pineapple: 1½ cups

Blanched almonds: 1 cup
Shelled pistachio nuts: ½ cup
Shelled filberts: 1 cup

FIRST: Break the large pieces of walnuts and pecans with the fingers. Cut the cherries in halves and the pineapple in small chunks. Halve the almonds, then thoroughly mix all the ingredients. Put a light coat of mineral oil on the marble slab and spread the mixture out in a cake about ½ inch thick. Use four ⅜-inch wooden sticks, if necessary, to make the sides of the cake straight and square; remove the sticks before finishing the candy.

Sugar: 2 cups
Water: 1 cup
Karo light corn syrup: 1 cup

Oil of orange: ½ tsp.
Orange food color

NEXT: In a medium-sized saucepan, place the first three ingredients. Stir until the sugar is suspended, then place on high heat, stirring until the sugar is all dissolved. Cook to 300°F. without stirring, then remove the pan from the burner. Add oil of orange and stir in well, at the same time stirring in enough orange food color to tint the syrup. As soon as the color and flavoring are well mixed, pour the syrup over the cake of fruit and nuts on the slab. Pour across and back and forth, making sure that the entire cake is covered with the syrup. Some will run down through the cake or flow out onto the slab at the sides of the cake. This should be cut off with a knife or the fondant scraper before it has entirely hardened.

Lightly wipe the top of the cake with mineral oil, applying it with your fingertips. Before the syrup hardens into crack, cut the cake in strips about ¾ inch wide, then into pieces about 1 inch long. When the candy is completely cool it can be broken apart and stored in an airtight container, or the pieces can be wrapped individually in squares of waxed paper.

About three weeks after this brittle is made, the hard crack will sugar out. This means it will turn opaque, and become slightly crumbly, instead of remaining clear and very hard. You may either wait until the sugaring-out stage or serve it freshly made.

While not strictly a brittle, and while not technically a hard-crack, our Butter Crunch falls into both these categories well enough to be included in this chapter.

Actually butter crunch is so delicious that it should have a chapter all by itself. It is also one of the richest of candies, and one of the most touchy to make. If you follow the recipe very carefully, however, you will have no trouble. Do not make any substitutes, especially in the kind of pan for cooking the candy. *This is of the greatest importance.* If the pan is not the correct kind, weight, and is not heat-retaining, the butter and sugar will separate and you will be able to do nothing with the result but discard it. With a regular pan, the metal is hottest on the bottom directly over the heat. The candy boils at this point. As it is stirred up, it will alternately boil and chill. After a few minutes of this treatment, the candy will revolt, and you will end up with a mass of cooked sugar globs floating in boiling butter.

The next thing that often gives beginners trouble is the matter of stirring. The agitation of ingredients in candymaking is important. I have described the stirring motions to use when making fondant. These have been worked out, not to complicate matters, but because they are a very necessary part of producing the sugar chemistry in the making of different kinds of products. In the case of butter crunch, the stirring must be *constant.* By this I mean that you may not stop for any reason whatever from the time you start until the candy is done. It must be rapid, and thorough. ALL of the sugar must be kept in motion in ALL of the butter. Therefore, you must make certain to have your stirring cover the entire bottom of the pot. When the candy begins to thicken, it will become "cheesy" in texture, and the stirring merely tends to move the mass about on the bottom of the pot. At this point stir with a folding motion to insure that all parts of the candy mass are being cooked evenly.

The nuts used in the *center* of butter crunch should be coarsely chopped. Using a large knife on a board is the best way to do this. The nuts for the *outside* should be very finely chopped. You cannot grind the nuts in a food chopper, since this would extract the oil from them, and you would end up with a pasty mass. A food blender will do the job if you are careful not to leave the nuts in the machine too long. Otherwise, the only thing to do is chop, chop, chop on the board with the knife. To give you courage, I can tell you that the end result of making butter crunch is worth all the time, effort and trouble you go through to get it.

BUTTER CRUNCH

Butter (or margarine): 1 lb.
Sugar: 2 cups
Karo light corn syrup: 1 Tbsp.

Salt: ¼ tsp.
Coarsely chopped walnuts: 1 cup

Coating:

Finely chopped walnuts: 1 lb.
Vanilla-Sweet Chocolate Coating, tempered, or

Milk Chocolate Coating, tempered

For home manufacture of butter crunch, the pan to use is either a heavy cast-iron Dutch oven, or a large, heavy cast-iron frying pan. Griswold is a good make for both, and you can find them in hardware stores, department stores and houseware departments. DO NOT SUBSTITUTE ANY OTHER KIND OF PAN. The new enamelled cast-iron pots imported from Belgium, Sweden and other countries, and coated in bright and cheery colors are *not* suitable. They are too light in weight and will not distribute the heat evenly enough. The old-fashioned black iron pots and skillets are the best ones to use.

With the above cautions out of the way, we can melt the butter in the pan, over a high heat, then add the sugar slowly, stirring all the time. From now on you may not stop the stirring.

When the mixture boils, add the Karo syrup and cook, to 290°F., stirring constantly. Add the salt and the coarsely chopped nuts and stir in well, then pour the candy out on the well-buttered marble slab, very quickly spreading it thin as it hardens quite rapidly. To assist in spreading it, have your fondant scraper handy, with the blade buttered. This, together with the back of the wooden stirring spoon, will do the job.

As soon as the candy has hardened, lift it from the slab with the fondant scraper. Try to keep it in as large pieces as you can; if it does break up into smaller pieces, it makes it a bit harder to coat it. The candy will be just as delicious.

Place the finely chopped walnuts in a wide, shallow tray, and pour the tempered chocolate in another. Pick up a piece of crunch, lay it in the chocolate and then coat it all over with the fingers. Avoid getting the chocolate thick on some areas and thin on others, but make an even coating all over. Lay the chocolate-coated piece on top of the nuts, then lift and sprinkle nuts all over the top, and on all edges. If you use both hands to coat the crunch, an assistant will have to work the nuts for you, since you would otherwise transfer the nuts to the chocolate. Shake off all loose nuts and lay the pieces on waxed paper for the chocolate to harden. After this has taken place, the large pieces may be broken into manageable pieces and the candy stored in flat tin boxes between layers of waxed paper.

I prefer personally to use milk chocolate in coating butter crunch, but it does do well with the regular Vanilla-Sweet Chocolate coating, too. This candy will keep well as long as it is stored in tightly sealed boxes, in a cool place.

Making Coconut Candies, Clusters and Cups

That most people like coconut candy is evidenced by the popularity of Mounds Bars and other commercial coconut candies. Here is a coconut bar that is unique in flavor. Very easy to make, it uses coconut in the form of very fine shreds, called "macaroon coconut" by bakers' and confectioners' supply houses, for the simple reason that it is used in this form to make macaroons.

COCONUT ROYAL BARS.

PART 1:

Macaroon coconut: 1½ lbs.
Candied cherries, chopped: ½ lb.
White raisins: ½ lb.

Shelled pecans, chopped: ½ lb.
Candied pineapple, chopped:
  ½ lb.

PART 2:

Karo light corn syrup: 3 cups
Sugar: 2 cups

Water: 1 cup

PART 3:

Macaroon coconut, toasted: 1 lb.

Vanilla-sweet chocolate coating
  (p. 31)

Begin by toasting the pound of coconut called for in Part 3. Select a large kettle with a wide, flat bottom, or a large cast-iron frying pan and place over medium heat. When hot, put in the coconut and stir constantly with a wooden spoon until the coconut is an even light brown color. Place in a large bowl to cool.

PART 1: Place all the ingredients in Part 1 of the recipe into a large kettle and mix thoroughly with a wooden spoon. Set aside temporarily.

PART 2: Into a medium-sized saucepan, place the ingredients in Part 2 of the recipe. Stir until the sugar is in suspension, then place on high heat and continue to stir until the sugar is completely dissolved. Cook to 236°F. without further stirring, then pour the syrup over the mixture (Part 1) of coconut, fruits and nuts. Mix all together completely until it forms a paste.

The bar paste is packed with a rolling pin between wooden or metal slab bars.

After packing tightly, cut the paste into individual bars with a heavy knife.

After lightly oiling the marble with mineral oil, make a square form on the marble slab with metal slab bars or use four wooden sticks about ⅜ inch thick. Pack the mixture (Parts 1 and 2) into this form, evenly and compactly. The resulting cake should be no higher than the thickness of the sticks—⅜ inch. Allow the cake to stand until it is completely cool, then remove the sticks and, with a large knife, cut it into bars about an inch wide and two inches long. Turn each piece upside down on a sheet of waxed paper as it is cut and let the bars stand for 3 to 4 hours.

PART 3: *Covering*—The bars are to be dipped and rolled in coconut. Prepare the melted and tempered coating chocolate (Chapter 3) and set out the big dish of previously prepared toasted coconut, ready for use. Dipped candy that is to be rolled in a covering of some sort is handled a bit differently from dipped Chocolate Creams. In covered candy it does not matter so much if your hands sweat, except that the chocolate remaining after dipping may streak and not be useable for regular dipping. If your hands sweat (see test, page 35), wear a pair of surgical rubber gloves, obtainable in almost any drug store, when dipping covered candies. These gloves fit the hands snugly and are so thin that you will still have the feel of whatever you are doing, yet they will prevent dampness from the hands from reaching the chocolate. Gloves cannot be worn while dipping Chocolate Creams or any other candy that must be coated, laid out on dipping paper and topped with a "string" of chocolate because the rubber gloves plus the chocolate make the candy so slippery that it is impossible to control the dipping.

METHOD: To dip these bars, all that is needed is to get enough melted chocolate around the bar to allow the toasted coconut to stick to it. The chocolate, serving only as an adhesive, should not be a thick coating. Pour out a small amount of melted chocolate on the marble slab. (Be sure first to clean off the oil put on it for making the candy!) Be careful not to drip water from the pan into the chocolate—wiping the pan off before pouring is a necessary precaution. Temper the chocolate with one hand until you cannot feel any warmth from it, and you are ready to dip. Drop a bar into the chocolate, then pick it up with your dipping hand and rub chocolate over the entire surface to make sure that there are no spots left uncovered. Such spots are called "holidays" and will allow the center to dry out if they are present. Wipe the coated bar out of your dipping hand into the dish containing the toasted coconut, then with your other hand, cover the bar, roll it around for a bit, remove it from the coconut and shake most of the surplus coconut off before laying the finished bar on a sheet of waxed paper.

As you progress, you will find that it is very easy to dip one bar while you are rolling another. As you put the first bar into the toasted coconut, drop a second into the chocolate and work both bars at the same time. Every time you take a bar out of the toasted coconut, you have a new one coming out of the choco-late, and as you drop this one, you can put a new one into the chocolate. The work will go very rapidly, once you get the knack of it. Just be sure that there is not a *thick* layer of chocolate on the bars, because if there is, as you roll the outside of the bar in the coconut, it will sink into the chocolate and you will not have a covered surface, but a sticky chocolate one, making the bar very messy to handle and eat. It will also destroy the nice appearance of the finished candy.

The shelf life is very long for Coconut Royal Bars. Shelf life means the length of time a candy can remain fresh and edible. These bars will keep for many, many weeks, as fresh as the day they were made.

CLUSTERS

Now that you have used chocolate coating for the first time, there are several things you could do with the leftover chocolate after the bars have been covered. Here are some ideas.

RAISIN CLUSTERS

Melted chocolate coating: 1 cup
(more or less)

Seedless raisins: 1 lb. *or*
White raisins: 1 lb. *or*
Raisins, white, seedless: ½ lb. of
each, mixed

The chocolate must be retempered as described in Chapter 3. When it is at dipping temperature, add the raisins and stir them into the coating. With a teaspoon drop small quantities onto a sheet of dipping paper or a sheet of waxed paper laid on a sheet of corrugated cardboard or thin plywood. Let stand until they are hard, and the candy is ready to use.

PEANUT CLUSTERS

Tempered chocolate: 1 cup

Roasted peanuts: 2 cups

Temper chocolate. When at dipping temperature, add peanuts. Mix together and drop with a teaspoon as in the raisin clusters. Any kind of peanut may be used. If you use large "goober" peanuts, they should have "skins" removed. The small Spanish peanuts may retain the skins. Only roasted nuts should be used, and they may be salted or not, according to your taste.

Variations: Try other kinds of nuts, such as broken pieces of pecans or walnuts. Filberts, too, can be used whole, three or four of them making a cluster. You can also mix nuts and raisins. Candied fruits are not good to use because they will ooze a syrup that will break down the chocolate, making the candy clusters sticky and difficult to handle.

CUPS

Metal foil candy cups may be filled with chocolate, and a variety of good things embedded in the centers. While the best coating for candy cups is milk chocolate, you can use the regular vanilla-sweet chocolate coating if you like a darker chocolate. For cups, candied fruits are quite useable, if they are embedded deep enough to keep well within the chocolate. In any case, candy cups are eaten by peeling the cup off the chocolate without handling the piece itself, so even if it is a bit sticky it is not messy to handle.

Separate the foil cups and put a small quantity of melted chocolate in the bottom of each. Then drop in the center. It may be a candied cherry, a small piece of candied angelica or candied fruit, pineapple, citron, orange or lemon peel; or try a whole filbert or a small dab of peanut butter. If you are using milk chocolate, any number of centers may be used in a candy cup. Always make sure that, especially with the dab of peanut butter, there is space all around the sides of the center for the chocolate to flow in. The center filling should be completely embedded in the middle of the chocolate coating, not up against one side of the foil cup. Fill cup to the top with chocolate.

Each cup may be topped with a tiny sugar decoration, one silver dragée, a crystallized rose or violet petal or any other desired decoration. They make especially festive candies when dressed up in this fashion.

Making Fine French Creams

Do you think you have handled enough sugar and chocolate now to try your hand at making some chocolate creams? All right, let's get on with it . . .

While you can make the centers of your chocolate creams

French Creams are easy to make and unusual, too.

any shape you wish, it has become common practice to make certain flavors in certain shapes, just as it has become common practice to combine certain nuts with certain flavors, certain colors with certain flavors. I will chart these combinations for you here, and you may either use the chart or develop your own combinations.

FLAVOR-SHAPES OF CENTERS

Vanilla .... round balls
Chocolate .... round balls
Coffee .... oval balls
Orange.......................... round balls
Lemon .... oval balls
Cherry .... round balls, flattened *very* slightly
Strawberry .... oval balls
Pistachio..................... oval balls
Rose .... small round balls
Violet .... small oval balls
Bonbons .... round balls
Peppermints .... flat patties—round balls, flattened

The very names of the different flavors will tell you what colors they should be: pistachio should be pale green, and cherry should be a darker red than is strawberry. The vanilla center is not colored. Peppermint patties are colored a little darker green than is pistachio. Wintergreen patties should be colored pink.

It is a fact that psychology plays a large part in the enjoyment of the things one eats. A piece of candy with a nicely colored center tastes much better than the same piece would if the center were not colored according to the flavor. A vanilla piece, for example, would *taste* terrible if, when you bit into it, you found the center a brilliant orange. Blue is a color that is least palatable. Try to think how much blue candy you see, or blue cakes or cookies? Not very many. There are blue jellybeans, but only infrequently, and once in a while you may see a pale blue gumdrop. Can you imagine what a Strawberry Chocolate Cream with a bright blue center would taste like? And, yet, if you closed your eyes when eating the candy, it would be delicious. This is a factor that has been taken into consideration over a period of many years and has set the standards for food colorings.

One time, as a Hallowe'en joke, I made up some Chocolate Creams. Flavoring several basic batches of fondant centers differently, I divided each batch in half, and colored one half with the color matching the flavor; the other half was colored terrible shades of blue, gray, brown—any mixture of deep and bilious colors I could mix. I put the colored ones on one plate and the regular ones on other plates. Then, as friends would drop in, I would offer a piece of the wrong-colored candy to them. Without exception, as soon as they bit into the chocolate and saw the color of the remaining piece, they would make a face and say "Ich," or "Ugh," and spit it out. "That tastes terrible," most would exclaim. Then I would apologize, telling them I had offered them my joke candy, and present the "good" chocolates, in the same flavor as they had just rejected. The usual comment would be, "This is more like it," and they would enjoy the candy. There was absolutely no difference in the taste, and the two cases in which the test failed were those who popped the entire piece into their mouths and ate it without seeing it! So much for the power of sight influencing taste. One person asked me about a lemon cream colored a bright deep blue: "What did you flavor it with, ink?" I never told them the secret.

Nuts, like coloring, have been standardized, and the combinations follow.

FLAVOR COMBINATIONS WITH NUTS

Vanilla .... English walnuts
Orange .... pecans
Lemon........................ coconut
Cherry........................ almonds
Pistachio .... pistachio
Strawberry .... filberts

These combinations are used in making Chocolate Creams with nutted centers, or in making French Creams with chopped nuts on the outsides of the candies. The same combinations are used in making plain-center Chocolate Creams decorated after dipping with a nut or a piece of nut on the top. Brazil nuts are not used in cream centers of Chocolate Creams, for they are so oily that they break down the fondant and thin out the chocolate when the candy is rolled in them. About the only time I use Brazil nuts is to make them into milk-chocolate-covered nuts. Coffee and chocolate centers of Chocolate Creams are always left plain, but the tops may be decorated, or the French Creams rolled in chocolate sprinkles, which come in two types—light and dark. The Coffee Creams are matched with the dark sprinkles, and chocolate centers matched with light ones. (Sprinkles are also called chocolate jimmies, in some parts of New England. The trade sells them as chocolate rice or as decorettes.)

To give you still more experience in handling fondant and chocolate, I want to teach you how to make French Creams before we get to plain Chocolate Creams. Paradoxically, French Creams, which are the real elite of the candy family, are much easier to make for the beginner than are regular Chocolate Creams. This is because the chocolate is covered with concealing materials and you need not be an expert dipper in order to turn out very creditable pieces. In other words, beginner's mistakes are hidden when you make French Creams.

In the recipes calling for fondant, the kind of fondant used is Recipe Number 1 (p. 46), the milk-and-butter fondant. You may use either the one with cream of tartar or the one with corn syrup used as the "doctor." If you are using this book in the manner of a student using a text book, then you will already have made up a batch or two of center fondant and have it ripening in the refrigerator. If you are reading the book first, to familiarize yourself with candymaking in general, then you may return to Chapter 4 and make one or two batches of this fondant.

ADVANCE PREPARATIONS

Certain things must be prepared in advance when making French Creams. The nuts for coating the outside must be chopped. Chopped is literally what should be done with nuts.

They should *never* be ground, as this process presses the oil from the nuts, and they may turn into a paste. A piece of board, or a regular chopping board and a large stiff knife are the tools to use for chopping nuts. A small pile is placed on the board, and, with one hand firmly hold the point of the knife down on the chopping board, lift the handle and swing the knife up and down on the nuts, chopping through them. Continue to chop, moving the handle of the knife in an arc, never allowing the point end of the knife to lift from the board. Keep the pile scraped together, as it will tend to flatten and spread out all over the board. Make the strokes slow and steady; a fast stroke can scatter the nuts all over the kitchen.

Nuts for coating French Creams should be chopped to about the size of rice grains. The actual size is hard to specify, since rice grains are long and thin, while the nut pieces will be chunky. However, the simile will give you an idea of the *bulk* of the pieces of nuts, if not the shape. Do not make them too fine, or the tiny pieces will embed themselves into the chocolate coating. In order to chop filberts successfully, first cut them into two or three pieces with a small paring knife while holding the nut in your fingers. Then put the cut pieces on the board to finish chopping with the big knife.

Macaroon coconut for coating lemon-flavored French Creams should be rubbed between the hands to make sure that the coconut is separated. It should be fine and dry, loosely shredded, before using. When nuts are chopped, and the coconut loosened, store each variety in a tightly sealed jar, ready for use.

The chocolate used for dipping is vanilla-sweet, or the dark coating chocolate. Milk chocolate can be used, if desired, but the creams are better if darker chocolate is employed.

Use xxxx powdered sugar to prevent the fondant from sticking to the marble slab, and to your hands as you work it to make the centers. The sugar should be sifted free from lumps, and the marble must be completely dry before lightly sifting on the sugar.

The desired quantity of fondant is taken from the storage container and put on the slab. A dent is made in the center with a thumb or finger, into which is measured the correct quantity of flavoring, and also the food coloring. These ingredients are worked into the fondant simultaneously, kneading it until the color is perfectly distributed throughout, with no streaks. As you work the flavor into the fondant, try to keep the flavor from running off the fondant onto the marble, since some of the volatile flavoring will soak into the pores of the marble, flavoring *it* and losing the benefit of the flavor in the fondant. This is especially true of the very strong oils such as oil of peppermint, orange and lemon. Oil of cassia is perhaps the worst, since, if you should spill that on the slab, after working up that flavor of fondant you will have to scrub the slab to keep the cinnamon from flavoring the next batch.

After the flavor and color are mixed in, form the fondant into a ball and put it aside on a piece of waxed paper to stand until all the other flavors you are going to make at this time are completed. At the end, scrape off the marble slab with the fondant scraper, making it as clean as possible, but do not use any water in cleaning it. Dust the working area lightly with xxxx powdered sugar, exactly as you would use flour before rolling out a pie crust. Do not use much powdered sugar, since the fondant will take it up, making the fondant dry and mealy if too much is present.

The ball of mixed fondant is now rolled out into a "rope" about ½ inch in diameter. If the amount of fondant you are using is too much to be rolled into the rope at one time, divide it and roll part of it. Make that part up into centers, and then work the remainder.

There is a small trick to rolling fondant. If you put a lot of down-pressure on the candy as you roll the rope, the center will become hollow, and you will end up with a collapsed tube of fondant. This is obviously undesirable. The rolling should be done with the hands held flat, the fingers held together. Apply only enough pressure to keep the fondant moving under your hands. You should start at the center of the rope, working your hands out toward the ends as you roll. This will pull the fondant sideways, instead of mashing it down on the marble and the rope will remain solid. If, the first time you roll out a rope it is uneven—large in some places and skinny in others—ball up the fondant in a firm lump and start again. You can do this several times before drying out the fondant too much.

Dust the insides of your hands with powdered sugar to pre-

Roll the fondant into a rope, with the fingers pulling away from each other.

vent them from sticking to the fondant. You will note that the
heat of your hands will tend to soften the fondant considerably,
and, if you continue to handle it for a long period of time, the
surface of the fondant will actually become damp and sticky,
making the rope stick to the marble slab and to your hands.
Therefore avoid keeping your hands in contact with the fondant any longer than is necessary to form the rope.

If, after taking it from the storage container and mixing the
color and flavor, the fondant is very soft and sticky, a small
quantity of xxxx powdered sugar may be mixed into it to dry it
enough to permit working into the centers. If the fondant is
crumbly and dry, a *tiny* amount of water may be added to
soften it—never more than ¼ teaspoon at one time. Work this
in well, then pinch the fondant to see if it has a nice workable
texture. If it is still dry and mealy, add another ¼ teaspoon of
water and work it in.

After the rope is rolled out correctly to its ½-inch diameter,
and is as even along its whole length as you can get it, with the
fondant scraper or an ordinary table knife chop it into individual pieces about ½ inch long. This will make a center about

½-inch in diameter, which is plenty large enough for French Creams, since the outer diameter will be increased by the addition of the chocolate coating and the nuts.

Following the table of Flavor Shapes, on page 84, shape the individual centers.

A very light pressure is all that is needed to roll a center. If you put too much pressure on the fondant between your hands, two things will happen. It will get soft and sticky, suddenly sticking to both of your hands, and/or it will not roll into a round ball, but take the shape of two blunt cones with the bases together.

Using practically no squeeze pressure between your hands, the center will quickly roll out into a nice marble-shaped ball, and you can drop it on the paper. To make oval balls, first roll it into a round ball, then with the hands making a straight instead of a circular motion, make one or two passes to shape the ball into an oval. Set them in rows on a sheet of waxed paper placed on a sheet of corrugated cardboard or thin plywood. Make the rows at least an inch apart so you can pick up any center without mashing those adjacent to it. After all the cen-

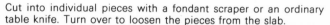

Cut into individual pieces with a fondant scraper or an ordinary table knife. Turn over to loosen the pieces from the slab.

Roll the pieces between the palms, keeping the hands dusted with powdered sugar to prevent sticking.

ters are rolled, put the trays holding them aside to allow a thin crust to form on the fondant. A couple of hours should be sufficient. After they have a nice crust, lift each center off the waxed paper. As you lift the center from the paper, you will note a wet spot where it was. Do not put the center back upon a wet spot. Turn it upside down and place it back on the paper in a different spot. This is another reason to place your rows of centers an inch apart at the beginning—to allow enough space for turning them onto a dry area. The bottoms of the centers will be flat. Leave them flat. Do not make any attempt to shape the fondant centers as you pick them up, or you will break the crust. Handle them gently. Allow the trays of centers to stand once more until the crust has formed over the damp flat bottom, then they are ready for dipping.

Since, after turning, all the centers will be loose on the waxed paper, be extra careful when picking up a tray of them or they may roll off onto the floor. Returning to Chapter 3 for review of the directions for handling the chocolate, tempering it and getting it ready on the marble slab for dipping. In the following directions, I will assume you to be dipping by hand,

After the top has formed a light crust, the centers should be turned
over to permit the bottoms to dry.

although the same instructions will also apply to fork dipping,
if you bear in mind that the tapping process is slightly different
to avoid squashing the center down between the tines of the
dipping fork.

DIPPING DIRECTIONS

I will give here the directions for dipping before the flavor
and nut combinations of the French Creams, since the tech-
nique for dipping them all is identical.

IF YOU ARE RIGHT-HANDED: Place the chocolate in the center of the marble slab, then place a sheet of centers to the right
side of the chocolate, a bit toward the far side of the puddle. To
the left, toward the far side of the chocolate, place a shallow
dish containing the chopped nuts or other material with which
the particular center is to be coated. Also to the left, directly
forward of the dish of nuts, place a sheet of corrugated cardboard or thin plywood topped by a sheet of dipping paper or
waxed paper. For French Creams, this paper could also be

placed in a shallow low-sided baking pan.

You will be working cross-handed, for several reasons. It is not as clumsy as you may think. This method of placement makes it possible to drop the centers into the chocolate with no danger of carrying nuts into the coating. It also leaves your left hand free to work in the nuts without interfering with the dipping process.

IF YOU ARE LEFT-HANDED: Place the chocolate in the center, and the other three parts are reversed—the nuts at the right far side of the chocolate, the dipping paper on plywood or corrugated board to the right, forward, and the centers to the left far side of the chocolate.

You are now ready to start. Reach over the chocolate and pick up a center, dropping it into the chocolate. With the dipping hand (right or left) pick up the center and gently rub chocolate all over it, taking great care not to mash the center while doing so. Carry the coated center over to the dish of nuts and squeeze it out from your fingertips, letting it *drop* into the nuts. *Do not place the center in the nuts while it is still in your dipping hand.* If you do so, the chances are that the center, with its bottom half covered wih chopped nuts, will stick to your fingers. Then, when the dipping hand goes back to the chocolate to pick up the next center, you will drop the first one, nuts and all, into the chocolate. This is not as impossible as you might think, since, with melted chocolate covering your dipping fingers, you may not even feel the center is still stuck to them!

As you drop the center into the nuts, reach over the chocolate, pick up a new center and drop that into the chocolate. While you are picking the center up in your dipping hand to repeat the coating process, with your other hand push the chopped nuts over the first center, pick it out of the nuts gently, letting all loose nuts drop off without trying to shake them off and deposit that center on the dipping paper. As you are putting the nutted center on the dipping paper, you will be reaching out to drop the second center into the dish of nuts. After placing the center on the dipping paper, tap any loose nuts off your fingers, reach over and pick up a third center, dropping it into the chocolate. You are now well into your production line, and your motions from now on will be alternately crossing over the

Several centers may be dropped into the nuts at one time before rolling them.

chocolate puddle adding new centers and disposing of coated ones.

It is easy, once you realize what you have to do, but I would suggest you read these instructions over a couple of times until you are sure we are communicating. It would even be a good idea for you to make a couple of "dry runs." Pretend to pick up a center and drop it into the chocolate. Make a few motions over the chocolate and pretend to drop the center into the nuts. Carry this pantomime through the end, going through the motions of dipping two or three centers. You might find that a tray should be moved an inch or two one way or the other to make it easier for you to reach.

After you have filled the dipping paper with finished centers, it should be removed from the work area, placed in a flat, cool secure spot, and a new tray with a fresh dipping paper placed in position. As the tray of centers is emptied, a new tray can be placed right on top of the old one, without having to find a spot to put the empty tray.

When the creams have hardened, they can be picked up, lightly shaken to knock off all nuts that are not stuck to the chocolate, then dropped into individual candy cup and packed away for storage.

If you are dipping in the heat of the summer, you must have some method of keeping the chocolate cool after the centers are dipped. This is especially true of plain Chocolate Creams, where the entire outside of the candy is coated with chocolate. This coating will streak if it gets too hot or humid while dipping. In the summer it is best to dip at night when it should be a little cooler, and, when you start the operation, clear off a shelf in the refrigerator where the tray of dipped chocolates can be placed to cool while you are dipping the next tray. Do not leave the candy in the refrigerator for longer than 20 or 30 minutes, or it will become so chilled through that it will sweat when removed and *really* streak all over.

Here are the flavor-color-nut combinations for some varieties of French Creams:

VANILLA FRENCH CREAMS

Fondant (p. 46): 2 cups　　　　**Chopped English walnuts:**
Extra-strong vanilla extract: 3 tsps.　　**3-4 cups**

Combine fondant, flavoring and nuts, mix well. Roll round centers.

We immediately come to the flavor which is difficult to manage because of the large amount of vanilla extract needed to flavor the fondant. This amount of moisture will make the fondant very soft and gooey. A few things can be done to help this condition. Dry vanilla, ground from a vanilla bean may be used; the fondant can be flavored the day before using, and permitted to stand to harden up a bit, or xxxx powdered sugar can be added to dry it out a little. This last is not the best, since the amount of powdered sugar needed to counteract the softening action of the extract would make the centers quite mealy. On occasion I have used half dry grated vanilla and half liquid, with just a very small amount of powdered sugar added and let the fondant stand a long time unwrapped, to dry out. I make up the vanilla first of all the flavors I am going to work, then dip it last.

Powdered vanilla is used extensively in the manufacture of ice cream, and it may be purchased at bakery and confectioners' supply houses. No coloring is used in the vanilla centers.

ORANGE FRENCH CREAMS

Fondant (p. 46): 2 cups   Orange food color to suit
Oil of orange: ¾ tsp.   Chopped pecans: 3-4 cups

Combine ingredients, mix well, roll centers round.

LEMON FRENCH CREAMS

Fondant (p. 46): 2 cups   Yellow food color to suit
Oil of lemon: ¾ tsp.   Macaroon coconut: 3-4 cups

Combine ingredients, mix well, roll centers oval.

STRAWBERRY FRENCH CREAMS

Fondant (p. 46): 2 cups   Red food color to color light pink
Strawberry flavor: ¾ tsp.   Chopped filberts: 3-4 cups

Combine ingredients, mix well, roll centers oval.

CHOCOLATE FRENCH CREAMS

Fondant (p. 46): 2 cups   Light chocolate rice: 3-4 cups
Bitter chocolate: ½ to 1 oz.

The bitter chocolate should be grated into powder before using. It may be melted, and mixed into the fondant in that condition. This will tend to dry out the centers after they have been dipped, so you should add a small quantity of moisture to the fondant while working it. Try ½ teaspoon of water at a time, and make the fondant as soft as you can possibly work it, because it will stiffen up quite a bit in a short time after dipping. Roll the chocolate centers round.

CHERRY FRENCH CREAMS

Fondant (p. 46): 2 cups
Wild cherry extract: ¼ tsp.

Red food color to a dark pink
Chopped blanched almonds:
3-4 cups

Combine ingredients, mix well, roll centers round, flattening slightly.

COFFEE FRENCH CREAMS

Fondant (p. 46): 2 cups
Coffee flavor: 2-3 tsps.

Dash chocolate rice: 3-4 cups

Combine ingredients, mix well, roll centers oval.

Coffee flavoring is sometimes difficult to find in grocery stores, so, unless you are using the professional, strong flavors from supply houses, you can get a good coffee flavor by substituting 1 teaspoon of powdered instant coffee. The strong espresso kind is best, provided it is not freeze dried. (The freeze-dried powder is much too coarse to use for fondant flavoring.) G. Washington powdered coffee is next strongest to use for candy flavoring. If you use the powdered coffee, add ½ teaspoon of water to counteract the drying effect of the powder on the fondant. One teaspoon of the powder should be enough to flavor the batch, but you may like it stronger or weaker, so adjust it to suit your personal preference.

ROSE FRENCH CREAMS AND VIOLET FRENCH CREAMS

While these two flavors are truly French Creams, they are made without an outer coating over the chocolate, and thus will be included in the directions for plain Chocolate Creams (page 104). Rose and violet creams are probably the most unusual flavors to be found in chocolates. They are very seldom offered in America, and when they are found, are usually imported. Many persons turn up their noses when offered a rose or violet cream, but they are absolutely delicious. The flavor has a delicate perfume—once you have tasted them you will either love them or you will think they are terrible. There doesn't seem to be any intermediate degree of liking. Try them and see how you feel.

PISTACHIO FRENCH CREAMS

Fondant (p. 46): 2 cups
Pistachio flavoring: ¾ tsp.

Green food color to suit
Chopped pistachio nuts: 3-4 cups

Combine ingredients, mix well and roll centers to oval.

Some connoisseurs consider this flavor to be the ultimate in fine chocolates. Certainly it is very exotic and delicate, and, when made as a French Cream, with the outside coated with freshly chopped pistachio nuts, it adds a festive decorative note to a box or plate of chocolates.

8

Making Professional Chocolate Creams

Plain chocolates differ from French chocolates in that they are dipped in coating and left with the chocolate on the outside. These candies have a little thicker layer of chocolate on them, and a decorative swirl or string on the top. Sometimes they can be topped with a half pecan, or half walnut, or some other garnish. Usually, when the top is garnished, the centers are plain fondant. Chocolate Creams can be made with plain centers, or with nutted or fruited centers. The same combinations of flavors and nuts are used as are used in the French Creams (see page 85). I will give you two recipes for each flavor, one for plain centers, and the other for nutted centers. The treatment of the fondant is the same, and the rope-and-cutting and dipping are the same. The only difference is in the size of the rope.

VANILLA CHOCOLATE CREAMS

Fondant (p. 46): 2 cups   **Vanilla extract, double-strength: 3 tsps.**

Combine flavoring, mix well, roll centers round.

This flavor should be treated the same as I have mentioned in the French Cream list. The flavoring will make the fondant

Finished Chocolate Creams—they taste as good as they look.

so soft that you will have to thicken it by whatever method you choose of those offered. When the rope is rolled, make it about ¾ inch in diameter instead of only ½ inch in diameter. This, because the finished candy will be plain chocolate, and will not have the bulk of the nuts on the outside.

VANILLA-WALNUT CREAMS

Fondant (p. 46): 2 cups   **Vanilla extract double-strength:**
Chopped English walnuts: ½ cup   **3 tsps.**

Combine ingredients, mix well, roll centers round.

In this kind we do not have to worry about thickening the fondant so much, because the addition of the walnuts help to make it stiffer. If the fondant, after the nuts are added, is still too soft, a small amount of powdered sugar may be worked into it.

ORANGE CHOCOLATE CREAMS

Fondant (p. 46): 2 cups
Oil of orange: ¾ tsp.

Orange food color to suit

Combine ingredients, mix well, roll centers round.

ORANGE-PECAN CREAMS

Fondant (p. 46): 2 cups
Oil of orange: ¾ tsp.

Orange food color to suit
Chopped pecans: ½ cup

Combine ingredients and blend the nuts into the fondant. If they make the fondant too stiff, add about ½ teaspoon of water, no more, until this is well distributed. Roll centers round.

LEMON CHOCOLATE CREAMS

Fondant (p. 46): 2 cups
Oil of lemon: ¾ tsp.

Yellow food coloring to suit

Combine ingredients, mix well, roll centers oval.

LEMON-COCONUT CREAMS

Fondant (p. 46): 2 cups
Oil of lemon: ¾ tsp.

Yellow food coloring to suit
Macaroon coconut: ½ cup

Combine ingredients, mix well, roll centers oval.

The addition of finely shredded coconut to fondant tends to make the center dry out much sooner than normal. The addition of one tablespoon of Karo light corn syrup to the batch of fondant as you are working in the coconut, color and flavor will help keep the centers moist a lot longer. The addition of one teaspoon of glycerine will do the same thing.

PISTACHIO CHOCOLATE CREAMS

Fondant (p. 46): 2 cups   Green food color to suit
Pistachio flavor: ¾ tsp.

Combine ingredients, mix well, roll centers oval.

PISTACHIO NUT CREAMS

Fondant (p. 46): 2 cups   Green food color to suit
Pistachio flavor: ¾ tsp.   Chopped pistachio nuts: ½ cup

Combine ingredients, mix well, roll centers oval.

    The plain pistachio centers are very decorative when dipped
if, instead of placing the dipped cream on the dipping paper,
you stand it up slantingly on one end in a dish of finely chopped
pistachio nuts. This makes them look something like acorns,
with a gay cap of bright green nuts at one end. Just a few made
this way can be used to afford a decorative spot here and there
when packing a box of chocolates.

STRAWBERRY CHOCOLATE CREAMS

Fondant (p. 46): 2 cups   Red food color to color pink
Strawberry flavor: ¾ tsp.

Combine ingredients, mix well, roll centers oval.

STRAWBERRY-FILBERT CREAMS

Fondant (p. 46): 2 cups   Red food color to color pink
Strawberry flavor: ¾ tsp.   Chopped filberts: ½ cup

Combine ingredients, mix well, roll into ovals.

CHERRY CHOCOLATE CREAMS

Fondant (p. 46): 2 cups
Wild cherry extract: ¼ tsp.

Red food color to suit

Combine ingredients, mix well, roll into slightly flattened balls.

CHERRY-ALMOND CREAMS

Fondant (p. 46): 2 cups
Wild cherry extract: ¼ tsp.

Red food color to suit
Chopped blanched almonds:
  ½ cup

Combine ingredients, mix well, roll into slightly flattened balls.

You will note that these two kinds call for much less flavoring than did the ones before. This is because wild cherry extract, if you use the professional grades, is very strong, and will overpower the fondant if you use too much. If you are using household flavors, you may need more. Taste the fondant after the prescribed quantity has been well mixed in, add more if you wish a stronger flavor.

The following recipes for chocolate creams are given only once, because the ingredients used to identify them are not usually mixed in the fondant. All of these flavors make plain centers. Any decoration is indicated after the individual recipe.

COFFEE CHOCOLATE CREAMS

Fondant (p. 46): 2 cups

Coffee flavoring: 2 to 3 tsps.

Combine ingredients, mix well, roll into oval.

Powdered coffee can be used for flavoring this batch, as described in the French Cream section. To identify the center flavor after the pieces are dipped, a small pinch of chocolate rice—not more than six or eight grains—can be placed on top of each as it is put onto the dipping paper. Use the *dark* rice.

CHOCOLATE CREAMS

Fondant (p. 46): 2 cups   **Bitter chocolate: ½ to 1 oz.**

Flavor this fondant the same way as in making chocolate French Creams. Roll into round balls, and sprinkle six or eight grains of *light* chocolate rice on the top of each piece after it is dipped.

WINTERGREEN CHOCOLATE CREAMS

Fondant (p. 46): 2 cups   **Red food color to make a light**
Oil of sweet birch: ½ tsp.   **pink**

Combine ingredients, mix well, roll into balls, and flatten.

True oil of wintergreen can be used in place of the oil of sweet birch, or methyl salicylate, both in the same quantity as the oil of sweet birch.

ROSE CHOCOLATE CREAMS

Fondant (p. 46): 2 cups   **Red food color to make light red**
Rose flavor: ¼ to ½ tsp.   **Crystallized rose petals**

Roll the centers into round balls.As each piece is dipped, place a piece of crystallized rose petal on top of the cream.

VIOLET CHOCOLATE CREAMS

Fondant (p. 46): 2 cups   **Violet food color**
Violet flavor: ¼ to ½ tsp.   **Crystallized violet petals**

Combine first three ingredients, mix well and roll into ovals, then dip and garnish with a violet petal on top of each.

CHOCOLATE PEPPERMINTS

Fondant (p.46): 2 cups   **Green food color to suit**
Oil of peppermint: ¼ tsp.

Combine ingredients, mix well, roll into a fondant rope. Cut the rope into pieces larger than usual—half again as large is about right. Roll them into round balls, then flatten them between your palms. After dipping, they can be garnished with bits of crystallized spearmint leaves if desired, but these peppermints are so delicious that just plain is fine.

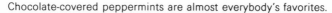

Chocolate-covered peppermints are almost everybody's favorites.

Making Candies with a Depositing Funnel

While this very useful tool was not described in the chapter on equipment, it is still a very good one to possess. You should come to know how to use it since, not only can you make quick candies with it, but you can reclaim leftover bits of coating fondant when you make bonbons, which you are sure to do some time or other.

Essentially, a depositing funnel is a funnel with a strong handle but without the usual long neck. They are used with a "depositing stick" or a "funnel stick." This is used as a valve to regulate or cut off the flow of fondant when depositing the individual pieces.

These funnels can be purchased in candy supply houses. Or, a funnel can be made by any competant sheetmetal worker, if you cannot get one from a company. However, Thomas Mills Manufacturing Company, 1301-15 North 8th Street, Philadelphia, Pennsylvania 19122 handles them, and is willing to sell through the mail, so it should not be a very great trouble to obtain one.

Cream Wafers, Wafer Mints and Cream Candies made in rubber molds (also obtainable from the Thomas Mills Company) are all made with the depositing funnel. Usually bonbon fondant is the material from which these candies are cast, because this fondant was designed for reheating and solidifying when coating bonbons. It hardens with a fine surface gloss, turns out of the mold very readily, and does not break up when handled, as would a milk-and-butter fondant.

HOW TO USE THE FUNNEL

Pour a quantity of prepared and melted fondant into the funnel with the stick put in place to close the opening. By raising and lowering the stick, you can deposit a measured amount of fondant either into the cavities of a rubber mold, on a rubber casting mat or on a piece of waxed paper. The fondant will harden when it cools, and it can then be removed from the mold or picked off the mat or paper, ready for consumption. The pieces may be coated with chocolate if desired, but they are probably better uncoated, since for Chocolate Creams the richer milk-and-butter fondant is more desirable.

A casting mat is very easy to make. Merely buy a small piece of rubber floor runner from a hardware store, the kind that comes in widths of 24 inches or more. It is sold from the roll by the foot. Purchase one with a surface composed of ridges, the kind designed to put down in hallways, on steps, or at the door

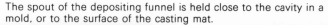

The spout of the depositing funnel is held close to the cavity in a mold, or to the surface of the casting mat.

The hardened cream wafers are pulled from the molds by turning
the cavity inside out with a fingertip.

affording a place to wipe your feet (or shoes) when entering the
house in inclement weather.

The rubber is very nearly the same kind used in molds and
fondant cast upon a piece of this mat will lift off cleanly and
remove easily, as it does from the molds. The bottoms of the
wafers cast on a mat are ridged, permitting them to be stacked
in boxes or on plates without sticking together.

The most common flavors used in making Cream Wafers in
this country are peppermint, wintergreen, orange and lemon.
However, there is no reason why some of the more exotic
flavors employed in making French Creams cannot be used for
the wafers. Rose and violet wafers are delicate, fragrant and
delicious as well as very unusual. Wild cherry, pistachio and
strawberry flavors are also uniquely good.

All molds or mats must be washed thoroughly, thoroughly
dried before casting fondant. Place two cups of coating fondant
in the top of a double boiler, placed over hot water on a medium
heat. When melted, flavoring and coloring of your choice is
stirred in. The funnel is immersed in a pot of very hot water to
preheat before being filled. Keep the funnel stop stick in place

to prohibit water from entering while funnel is heating. As soon as the funnel is hot, wipe it thoroughly dry and, with the stick again firmly in place, fill it by pouring in melted fondant.

Holding the end of the funnel about an inch or two above the mold, permit the hot fondant to flow into the cavity by lifting the stick barely enough to open the spout. Shut off the flow just before the cavity is entirely filled, since the stick will push out a little more fondant as it closes the spout. One or two trial castings will give you the "feel" of the stick. You should work as quickly as you can, because even with a preheated funnel, the fondant will cool quite rapidly, and become thick and sluggish.

Solidified fondant can be reheated to make it pour more easily, but care must be taken not to get it too hot. A teaspoonful of water added to the fondant will bring it back to the proper consistency. Fondant which has been brought to too high a temperature will turn color as it hardens. White spots may appear in the candies. When melting casting fondant, stir it frequently, and heat it only to the point where it becomes runny.

Making Beautiful Bonbons

Making bonbons is no more difficult than making Chocolate Creams. In place of being coated with chocolate, the pieces are dipped in bonbon coating fondant and a bonbon fork is employed instead of the fingers.

There are several ways of making bonbons. The coating fondant can be colored, but unflavored, the coating may be flavored *and* colored, while the centers can be plain, or they can be mixed with nutmeats or candied fruits. Since there is always a quantity of coating fondant left over after dipping any particular flavor of bonbon, I always color and flavor the coating, and use the remainders in the depositing funnel for making cream patties, as described in Chapter 9. In this way I get two kinds of candies out of one batch of fondant, in a manner of speaking.

Nutted centers dry out much faster than plain ones but the addition of a few chopped nuts so enhances the flavor sensation of a bonbon and, because these candies are not designed to be stored for weeks before being consumed, the more rapid drying-out is not objectionable.

The same nut-flavor-color combinations are used for bonbons as those for Chocolate Creams and French Creams. That is to say, orange-pecan, vanilla-walnut, etc. (See page 85.) The fondant is colored, flavored and rolled out exactly the same as for making chocolates, except that all bonbon centers, regardless of flavor, are rolled into round balls.

Nuts are not put *into* the coating fondant (page 59), but can be mixed into the center fondant (page 46). The coating fondant is melted in the top of the double boiler, over water brought to a boil and kept at a temperature just under boiling. Stir the fondant frequently, and color and flavor to suit while it is hot and melted. The coating in the double boiler top should be kept on the heat while dipping, in order to keep the fondant at the proper dipping consistency.

The bonbon fork is easy to use. Select one that has the loop about one-half as wide as the diameter of the bonbon center, in order to keep the center from slipping down inside the dipping loop, and also to make it possible to place the "crown" in the center of the top of the finished piece of candy. The fork is used only to manipulate the center once it has been dropped into the melted coating, to remove it from the coating pot and to place it on the waxed paper dipping sheet. Almost everyone will hold the fork at a slightly different angle, or use it in a slightly different manner. Therefore the dipping loop on the end of the fork should be adjusted so as to be perfectly flat when the bon-

Bonbons are delightful and are very easy to make.

bon is placed in position on the waxed paper. The end loop should be bent at an angle to fit your own particular dipping habit. Only then can you make a perfect and complete crown on the bonbon. The loop itself can be bent to take the curve of the top of a center, so that, in dipping, the loop wraps around the center and is in contact along its entire length and width.

DIPPING BONBONS

Roll the centers and place them in rows on a sheet of waxed paper which is, in turn, placed on a piece of plywood to permit easy handling. Let the centers stand until a light crust has formed on the surface, then turn all of them upside down to allow a crust form on the bottom as well. It is important to have this light crust on the centers to avoid undue distortion of the coating and center cream when dipping.

When all is ready, a clean sheet of waxed paper is placed on a second dipping board and positioned near the double boiler, convenient to your reach. The board of centers is placed on the other side of the boiler, and you are ready to go. Drop a center

The dipping fork may be steadied with the other hand, if necessary, while making the bonbon crown.

into the melted fondant, and immediately turn it over with the dipping fork to cover it completely with the coating. When you drop the center into the pot, put it in right side up. When you turn it over to coat it, the top will be down and you can then slip the fork under the piece and lift it out of the kettle.

Tap the fork *very* lightly on the side of the double boiler to dislodge any surplus coating, then draw it across the edge of the pot as you move it over to the waxed paper. This is to scrape the excess coating off the top of the bonbon, but great care must be taken not to scrape the top of the bonbon itself on the kettle. If you tapped the fork too hard, the center will have settled down inside the loop enough to stick out and be scraped off. If you tapped too lightly, there will be a quantity of surplus coating left in place, which will run down and make a blob around the bottom of the finished piece of candy.

The dipped bonbon is carried over to the waxed paper and the fork inverted to place the candy on its bottom. Hold the fork in contact with the bonbon for a few seconds after putting the piece in place, taking care not to push the candy around on the paper. Then, with a straight-up lift, pull the fork quickly off the bonbon, pulling the fondant up with it to make the distinctive "crown" that is the mark of a well-dipped bonbon. If you did not wait long enough to pull up the fork, the crown will sag back into the coating, disappearing and making a messy-looking piece. If you waited too long, the fondant will have hardened on the fork, and you will either pull the entire bonbon up off the paper, leaving the bottom coating stuck on the paper, or you will pull the top off the bonbon, leaving this part without any coating. Either way, the piece is a reject, since it cannot be dipped a second time. If this were attempted, the resulting piece would have a very thick coating on it, be much larger than the rest of the pieces, having too much coating fondant in pro-portion to the center fondant, making the piece too grainy. The best thing to do with ruined pieces like this is to use them as eating samples for anyone hovering around or, sample them yourself.

One or two trial dippings should be all that is needed to let you get the proper feel of the fork, and then it should be clear sailing.

Bonbons harden very quickly at room temperature, but they

should be permitted to stand for at least an hour or two before being removed from the dipping paper. This is because the surface hardens quickly, but it takes quite a bit longer for the coating to set completely on the bottoms.

Bonbons look best in white crinkle cups, and a quantity of these should have been separated and set out, ready for use when you pick the finished candy off the dipping paper. Lift the bonbon from the paper and drop it into a cup as quickly as possible, so that your warm fingers will not make spots on the sides of the candy. They are best lifted off the paper with a peeling motion to avoid the chance of pulling the bottoms off.

About the only decoration that looks well on bonbons is a single silver dragée not larger than ⅛ inch in diameter, or a very small sugar flower. These must be placed in position immediately after the bonbon is placed on the dipping paper, or the surface of the coating will have hardened sufficiently to prevent the decoration from sticking to the candy.

Such tiny sugar flowers can be purchased from candy and bakery supply companies. They are made with decorating tubes, and some of them are very lovely. They are usually sold

The crinkle candy cups must be separated from their stacks and set out individually.

on sheets of paper, from which they may be peeled when wanted. A quantity should be removed before you start to dip the bonbons, since there will not be enough time for you to deposit the coated candy, put the dipping fork down, peel off a flower and attach it, before the coating has hardened. It would be a smoother operation if you have a helper to put the decorations in place as you dip.

Bonbons should be stored in a cool place, the same as chocolates. They should be handled only by their crinkle cups, since warm fingers will make dull spots on the glossy coating of the bonbon. Bonbons make interesting additions to boxes of mixed candy, one or two being placed in each layer to break the monotony of only Chocolate Creams.

Following are some bonbon combinations. Others can be devised, limited only by your imagination and desire to experiment. Each recipe given here makes about 75 bonbons. All are made from the Center Fondant recipes on pages 46 and 47.

VANILLA BONBONS

French Cream Fondant: 2 cups

Vanilla extract: 3 tsps.

ORANGE BONBONS

French Cream Fondant: 2 cups
Oil of orange: ¾ tsp.

Orange food color to suit

NUTTED ORANGE BONBONS

French Cream Fondant: 2 cups
Chopped pecans: ½ cup

Oil of orange: ¾ tsp.
Orange food color to suit

FRUITED ORANGE BONBONS

French Cream Fondant: 2 cups
Candied orange peel, chopped:
 ½ cup

Oil of orange: ¾ tsp.
Orange food color to suit

LEMON BONBONS

French Cream Fondant: 2 cups   **Yellow food color to suit**
Oil of lemon: ¾ tsp.

COCONUT LEMON BONBONS

French Cream Fondant: 2 cups   **Oil of lemon: ¾ tsp.**
Macaroon coconut: ¼ cup   **Yellow food color to suit**

FRUITED LEMON BONBONS

French Cream Fondant: 2 cups   **Oil of lemon: ¾ tsp.**
Candied lemon peel, chopped: **Yellow food color to suit**
** ½ cup**

CHERRY BONBONS

French Cream Fondant: 2 cups   **Red food color to suit**
Wild cherry flavor: ¼ tsp.

FRUITED CHERRY BONBONS, 1

French Cream Fondant: 2 cups   **Wild cherry flavor: ¼ tsp.**
Maraschino cherries, chopped: **Red food color to suit**
** ½ cup***

FRUITED CHERRY BONBONS, 2

French Cream Fondant: 2 cups   **Wild cherry flavor: ¼ tsp.**
Candied cherries, chopped: ½ cup   **Red food color to suit**

---

*The difference between the first and second Fruited Cherry Bonbons lies in the fruit used. In the first recipe, the maraschino cherries should be patted dry between two paper towels after chopping. The fruit and fondant should be mixed, rolled out, and dipped as soon as possible, to finish the pieces before fondant begins to liquify. After dipping, centers will soften to a great degree, the process being initiated by the liquid remaining in the fibers of the cherries. Although this recipe has an excellent taste, it should be used only if the bonbons are to be consumed within a day or two of being made. Otherwise, coating fondant may liquify as well as centers.

STRAWBERRY BONBONS

French Cream Fondant: 2 cups   Red food color to suit
Strawberry flavor: ¾ tsp.

PISTACHIO BONBONS*

French Cream Fondant: 2 cups   Green food color to suit
Pistachio flavor: ¾ tsp.

NUTTED PISTACHIO BONBONS*

French Cream Fondant: 2 cups   Pistachio flavor: ¾ tsp.
Pistachio nuts, chopped: ½ cup   Green food color to suit

ANISE BONBONS*

French Cream Fondant: 2 cups   Black food color to suit
Oil of anise: ¼ tsp., scant

FLAVORS TO EXPERIMENT WITH

Bonbons lend themselves well to exotic flavors. Try some of the excellent synthetic flavorings available from candy and bakery supply houses. Peach is one, apricot another, while banana is one to try, but, unless you get *exactly* the right amount of flavor, the candy may taste like soap! Add the flavor one drop at a time, mixing it well into the batch of center fondant. After

---

*Anise and Pistachio Bonbons are strictly European, where they are gourmet delights. Pistachio Bonbons are especially the aristocrats of the bonbon family and, once you have tried them, the chances are you will be addicted to them. They are so good they are almost habit-forming. Anise Bonbons are also an unusual taste sensation, and are practically never found in the American market.

you have tasted it one time, your taste buds may not be reliable, and you should have other persons make the subsequent taste tests as you add the flavor. One tasting to a person. Keeping a record of how many drops you add to a measured batch of fondant will make it easier to duplicate the process when next you want to make that flavor. Write it in this cookbook beside the paragraph or below it.

Making Cordials and Liqueurs

When I was a boy, chocolate cordial cherries were one of my very favorite candies, especially if they were dipped in milk chocolate. They were also a great mystery to me. I dreamed up all kinds of fantasies about how they got the juice inside a closed globe of chocolate. I finally decided, after my first trip to the hospital for some now long-forgotten injury, that the miracle was accomplished by injecting the cherry juice into the chocolate with a hypodermic syringe. The small item of how to dip the cherry yet keep air all around it to allow space for the juice did not occur to me, fortunately for my peace of mind.

Cordial Cherries or Liqueur Cherries are another professional candy that can brought into the home kitchen and made with very little trouble. Candies made with alcoholic beverages cannot be made for sale in some states without a special license. However, there is nothing to prevent your making them at home for home consumption.

CORDIAL CHERRIES

Maraschino cherries are used in making cordials, and those with the stems retained are best for the liqueur candies. To make cordials, take as many cherries as you wish to use and drain them completely of their juice. Have the dipping chocolate (page 32) ready to use before starting the other operations, since in making cordials, speed is essential if you are to get the chocolate coating around the fruit before the cordialling begins.

Melt 2 cups of Center Fondant (page 46) in a double boiler top to dip one medium-sized jar of cherries. The fondant can be flavored with 1 or 2 teaspoons of the maraschino liquid if desired. Roll the drained cherries in a towel, then toss them for just a moment in powdered sugar to coat them well. Now dip them in the fondant the same as if you were dipping bonbons (page 112), except *do not* make a crown on the top. Turn them out of the dipping fork quickly onto a sheet of waxed paper.

As soon as all the fruits have been dipped in bonbon coating, they should be dipped in chocolate (pages 36, 41) previously put out for use. Some professional candymakers like to double-dip the bottoms, to make a thicker layer of chocolate on the bottom where the greatest chance of leakage occurs. To do this, take each dipped cherry and touch the bottom to the pool of chocolate, then place it on a dipping paper. When all the cherries have been bottom-dipped, the first ones should be hardened enough to dip them all over. (See pages 36, 41.) You must make

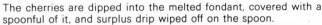

The cherries are dipped into the melted fondant, covered with a spoonful of it, and surplus drip wiped off on the spoon.

If brandied or rum cherries are being made, it is safer to double-dip the bottoms of the cherries.

very certain that an *even* thickness of chocolate covers the entire candy, or there will be a good chance of a leak occurring when the cordialling process begins.

In dipping cordials, the excess chocolate is tapped off the same as for dipping Chocolate Creams, but not quite so thoroughly. Keep it just a shade thicker. After all have been dipped in chocolate and set on dipping paper, set aside to cure for then the individual pieces are placed in crinkle cups and packed away to "cordial." This process will take from one day to three or four days, depending upon how much moisture was left within the cherry, and also on how thick the bonbon fondant was around the fruit.

The moisture inside the cherry "melts" the bonbon fondant inside the chocolate coating. A certain amount of pressure is engendered by the chemical process of liquifying, which is the reason for having the slightly thicker coating of chocolate on the piece, and the need for care in seeing that the center is evenly coated.

Often Cordial Cherries will cordial incompletely. That is, a small amount of fondant remains as fondant, and does not turn to liquid. Two reasons for this are easily corrected: you may have dried the cherries too much, and squeezed all the liquid out of their centers, not leaving in enough to cause cordialling; or the bonbon fondant coating may have been *too* thick.

Remedies for future use: keep the bonbon fondant thinner for the dipping or, if you like, add a teaspoonful of bonbon doctor to the melted fondant before dipping; also, dry the cherries a little less before the powdering prior to dipping.

RUM CHERRIES, BRANDIED CHERRIES

Rum or Brandied Cherries are delicious candies, and are made in the same way as cordialled cherries, with one difference: use the stemmed cherries and drain the liquid from their jar, leaving the fruit still inside. Now fill the jar with fine quality rum or brandy, replace the cap and let stand for a week.

At the end of that time, the cherries are treated in exactly the same way as if you were dipping plain Cordial Cherries; drain well, roll in powdered sugar, dip in bonbon coating (but this time do not add any flavor to the coating), coat the chocolate-bottoms then dip finally in chocolate. The stem is used as a convenient handle for the dipping processes, and is not coated past the point of attachment to the cherry. Make sure, when handling the candy, that you do not pull the stem or bend it so far that it breaks loose at the cherry, or you will have a leak at that point.

The cordialling process is a little faster with Rum Cherries than with Cordial Cherries. This is probably due to the alcoholic content of the liquid acting more rapidly on the fondant. At any rate, they should be fully cordialled within three days. Rum or Brandied Cherries should be kept in a cool place, to eliminate the possibility of pressure building up inside, which can reach the point of explosion, breaking the chocolate covering.

Notes on Crystallizing

Have you ever wondered how certain cream wafers, gumdrops, spice drops and many other candies were covered with a layer of sugar crystals? This professional method of finishing candy is so simple to do that it is a wonder every housewife doesn't already know how. Essentially, crystallizing is accomplished by "seeding" a super-saturated solution of sugar with the pieces you wish to crystallize. The recipe is very simple:

CRYSTALLIZING SOLUTION

Sugar: 3 lbs.   **Water: 2½ cups**

Cook to 221°F. *exactly,* stirring only until the sugar is dissolved. Place the pan of hot syrup where it will not be disturbed for 3 to 4 hours. Particular attention must be paid to the fact that the floor be steady, so the pan will not be shaken by anyone walking near it.

One or two thicknesses of clean, dry cheesecloth is now laid on the surface of the syrup. Tuck the edges down with a wooden spoon, to make certain the entire surface right up to the sides of the pan are covered. The cheesecloth should float on the surface, not be submerged under it.

I cannot stress the point too strongly that the pan must remain entirely undisturbed. If you bump it, hit the handle or in any other way jar the syrup you may as well pour it down the drain and start over, because in a short time you will probably have a solid cake of hard sugar with which nothing can be done!

While the syrup is curing, you can prepare the candy to be crystallized. You will need a couple of shallow rectangular glass dishes, such as Pyrex glass baking pans. A trivet must be made to fit the bottoms of the dishes. This is easy to do with a piece of ½-inch mesh hardware cloth which can be purchased at a hardware store. The ends and sides are bent down to make ½-inch or ¾-inch high walls, which will suspend the bed of the trivet that much above the bottom of the dish. Arrange the pieces on the trivet allowing not more than ¼ inch of space between pieces in every direction.

Put the dishes in a place where they, too, will not be jarred by anyone walking past, where they can remain completely undisturbed for at least 12 hours. When the syrup has cured, carefully peel the cheesecloth from the surface and discard it, not permitting it to drain back into the syrup. Carry the syrup over to the dishes, taking extreme care not to jar it or swish it around in the pot. From a low distance pour SLOWLY over the candy. *Do not let the syrup splash!*

Cover the pieces to a depth of from ½ inch to 1 inch. If any pieces float up as you pour, continue to pour until all the syrup is in, then with a fingertip push the floaters down and hold for a moment until they stay down. Usually the reason for floating is air entrapped on the piece.

Cover the dishes with anything that will keep dust out of them, and let them stand for at least 12 hours completely undisturbed. *Do not lift the covers* to see how the work is progressing. At the end of 12 hours (or overnight, which is a convenient time to crystallize candies), very gently lift one piece out of the solution, taking care not to splash the syrup, touch other pieces or make waves. Feel the wet piece of candy. If it is covered with a layer of fine hard crystals, the crystallizing is completed. If not, lay the piece back in its original position and let the tray stand for another 6 hours.

When the candy has a layer of crystals on it, remove the trivet loaded with the candy from the syrup. Balance it across the dish and permit it to drain thoroughly, for about 5 or 10 minutes.

Now remove each piece, placing it upside down on another clean trivet (made of hardware cloth the same as those for crystallizing), or on a cookie rack if the wires of the rack are close enough together to hold the candy without allowing it to fall through. After the candy has drained on the rack for an hour it should be turned over once again, placing each piece on another clean dry rack to permit the bottom surface to dry. When completely dry, the crystallized pieces will keep many times longer than they would if not coated.

Bonbons (Chapter 10) when crystallized are very professional looking; so are the Cream Wafers made with the depositing funnel (Chapter 9). Shapes made in rubber molds are perfect types for crystallizing. In point of fact, this is what those molds were made for—the manufacture of crystallized cream candies. Bonbons are especially good summer candies, for they do not melt as readily as chocolates, and they also add variety to boxes of chocolates, when mixed in.

A scoop filled with crystallized cream wafers, ready to serve.

Part Two

Some good
homemade candies

The fruit is filled with fondant from the tip of a table knife.

The filled fruit is rolled in plain or colored granulated sugar.

Homespun Candies,
Classics Among Homemade Candies

There are so many good home recipes for candy making that no book, even one that adapts professional recipes to the home kitchen, can ignore some of the classic recipes. Not because they are really easier to make than professional recipes, for many professional recipes are easier to follow than some of the home-style ones—but because they are familiar to so many people, because the product is good, the ingredients are easily obtainable in the usual supermarket or grocery store and, above all, because there is some thing nostalgic and satisfying about these recipes—these are the reasons we have collected and presented them here.

While a good part of this book is devoted to the making of professional-type candies at home, I have had so many requests while it was in preparation to include some old-fashioned favorites such as fudge, divinity, panocha, etc., that I am offering some of these recipes as an added section. These are candies I have made for years, and enjoyed fully. First, we shall begin with a couple of recipes for fudge that I have always extravagantly claimed to be the best fudge in the whole world!

CHOCOLATE FUDGE

Sugar: **4 cups**
Baking chocolate: **4 ozs.**, or
   Chocolate liquor coating: **4 ozs.**
Karo light corn syrup: **¼ cup**

Scalded milk: **1⅓ cups**
Butter or margarine: **¼ cup**
Vanilla extract: **2 tsps.**

Grate the chocolate, then melt it in the scalded milk, add the sugar and the corn syrup and bring to a boil, stirring until the sugar is dissolved. Cover the pan and boil for 2 to 3 minutes.

Remove the cover and cook to 236°F., stirring frequently. Slide the pan off the heat and add the butter. Leave the thermometer in the candy and allow the pan to stand undisturbed until the temperature drops to about 110°F.

Remove the thermometer, add the vanilla, then beat rapidly until the candy is very thick. Spread quickly into a well-buttered pan about ¾-inch deep and set aside to cool thoroughly. Cut into squares, remove from pan with buttered table knife and place upside down on a cookie rack or plate to dry.

CHOCOLATE NUT FUDGE

To the recipe for plain Chocolate Fudge, add 1½ cups of coarsely broken walnuts when the vanilla is added. The nuts may be chopped, but are much better if they are merely broken between the fingers. If walnuts are not available, pecans may be substituted, but walnuts are far better for this candy.

Beat as before and spread in a ½-inch deep 8-inch square pan and cut into small squares as before. Dipped in milk chocolate, this recipe makes the most marvellous fudge-centered chocolates you ever had!

Another old time favorite is panocha. This is a kind of fudge, too, and can be treated in several ways to dress it up. Try one of our variations, too.

PANOCHA (PENUCHE)

Brown sugar: 2½ cups
Butter or margarine: 1 Tbsp.
Karo light corn syrup: 1 Tbsp.
Milk: ¾ cup

Salt: a good pinch
Vanilla: 1 tsp.
Walnuts, broken: ½ cup

Combine all ingredients except nuts and vanilla; cook to 236°F., stirring until the sugar is dissolved. Slide pan from the heat and permit the candy to cool until the thermometer registers about 110°F. Add the vanilla and beat until the candy begins to thicken. Add the nuts and very quickly spread into a buttered 8-inch square pan. Cool and cut into ¾-inch squares, lifting them out and inverting them on a cookie rack to dry.

MOLASSES PANOCHA (PENUCHE)

Use the above recipe but substitute 2 tablespoons dark or black-strap molasses for an equal quantity of the milk. (Measure milk, take out 2 tablespoonfuls.)

SEAFOAM

Sugar: 2 cups
Karo dark corn syrup: 1 cup
Brown sugar, firmly packed: 1 cup
Water: ½ cup

Cider vinegar: 1 tsp.
Egg whites, beaten dry: 2
Vanilla extract: 1 tsp.
Walnuts, broken: 1 cup

Combine sugar, corn syrup, water and vinegar and cook in a covered pot for about 5 minutes, then remove cover and cook to 265°F. Cool slightly, then pour syrup over the beaten egg whites and beat vigorously until candy is very stiff.

Cool until just lukewarm (about 110°F.), stirring occasionally. Then add the vanilla and nuts and mix in thoroughly. Drop from a buttered teaspoon on waxed paper or a buttered cookie sheet.

DIVINITY

Sugar: 3 cups
Karo light corn syrup: 1 cup
Water: ½ cup
Cider vinegar: 1 tsp.

Egg whites, beaten dry: 2
Vanilla extract: 1 tsp.
Walnuts, broken: 1 cup

Place the sugar, corn syrup, water and vinegar in a pot and stir until the sugar is dissolved. Cover and cook over medium heat for 5 minutes. Remove the cover and cook to 260° to 265°F. (If the weather is dry, cook to 260°F. If it is damp and rainy outside, cook to 265°F. Remove pan from the heat and allow to cool for a few minutes, then pour the syrup over the beaten egg whites and beat vigorously until the mixture is very stiff. Cool until lukewarm (about 110°F.).

Add the vanilla and the nuts, mixing them in well. Then drop from a buttered teaspoon on waxed paper or a buttered cookie sheet.

BUTTERSCOTCH

Sugar: 2½ cups
Water: ¾ cup
Karo light corn syrup: ½ cup
Salt: ½ tsp.

Honey: ¼ cup
Butter or margarine: ½ lb.
Rum-butter flavoring: ½ tsp.

Mix together first three ingredients and cook to 270°F., stirring until the sugar is dissolved. Then add the rest of the ingredients, and cook to 290°F., stirring constantly. Remove from the fire and pour out on buttered marble slab, inside caramel bars arranged to make a space about 12 to 16 inches. As soon as the candy is poured, close up the bars until the candy is about ¼ inch thick. Allow the butterscotch to set until firm enough to hold its shape, then remove the bars and with a knife score the sheet both ways to make ¾-inch squares. After scoring, let the candy stand until it is completely cold, then, turning the sheet over, break it into individual pieces. Wrap each piece in waxed paper for storage. Keeps for a very long time.

CHEWY BUTTERSCOTCH

Sugar: 2¾ cups
Karo light corn syrup: 1²/₃ cups
Cocoa butter: 2 Tbsps.
Butter or margarine: ¼ lb.

Water: ¾ cup
Rum-butter flavoring: ¼ tsp.
Oil of lemon: 8 to 10 drops
Heavy cream: 2 Tbsps.

Place all ingredients except the flavorings and cream in a pan and cook to 250°F., stirring constantly, then add the flavors and cream and stir in thoroughly. Pour out on buttered marble slab between buttered caramel bars. When cool, cut into squares and wrap each piece in waxed paper.

Saltwater taffy is one of the big attractions at seashore resorts. It has been popular for decades and seems likely to continue in its popularity for years to come. It isn't hard to make, and it is a project that can be joined in by several members of the family. In the famous resort of Atlantic City, New Jersey, saltwater taffy is sold by the thousands of pounds each summer. Many different companies make it there right in view of the customers, and each vies with the other in the number of flavors offered. The result is a myriad of flavors in a rainbow of colors. There seems to be no limit to what can be done with this homespun candy. The recipe given here is one that has been in use for a very long time.

SALTWATER TAFFY

Sugar: 2¼ cups
Karo light corn syrup: ¾ cup
Water: 1 cup
Corn starch: 3 Tbsps.

Butter or margarine: 2 Tbsps.
Salt: 1 tsp.
Flavoring: (See Table, p. 134)
Food coloring

Mix all the ingredients except the salt, flavoring and coloring in a large kettle and cook to 260°F., frequently stirring. Add the salt and stir in well, then add the flavoring and coloring chosen from the table below. Pour out on a buttered marble slab and allow to cool enough to handle comfortably.

Lift candy from the slab and pull it outward with both hands, folding it in half and pulling out thin each time, until the candy is silky and opaque. Then pull the ball of candy out into a rope about ½ inch in diameter, and cut off in 1½-inch lengths; wrap each piece in waxed paper. An assistant can do the cutting as you pull the rope, and a second helper can do the wrapping.

A few flavors for you to start with will be found in the table, together with the appropriate colors. Paste food colors should be used, and these are added as you start to pull, making sure the color is placed well within the blob of soft taffy so it does not smear over your hands. If, when being pulled, the candy tries to stick to your hands, a small pat of butter rubbed well into the palms will eliminate the trouble.

SALTWATER TAFFY

FLAVORS	FOOD COLORS
Cherry—¾ tsp. flavor	Red color
Strawberry—¾ tsp. flavor	Pink color
Peppermint—¼ tsp. oil of peppermint	Green color
Orange—¾ tsp. oil of orange	Orange color
Lemon—¾ tsp. oil of lemon	Yellow color
Lime—Scant ¼ tsp. oil of lime	Pale green color
Vanilla—4 tsps. vanilla extract	No color added
Anise—¼ tsp. oil of anise	Black color

Hardly anything need be said by way of introduction to pecan pralines. This easy-to-make standby is very popular in the South, where pecans flourish. Pecan pralines and pecan pie are the two most frequently offered desserts, and they are both justly famous, for they are delicious. Pralines can be stored for a good length of time if wrapped in waxed paper after they have cooled.

PECAN PRALINES

White sugar: 2 cups
Brown sugar, firmly packed: 1 cup
Water: 1 cup
Cider vinegar: 1 tsp.

Butter or margarine: 1 Tbsp.
Pecans, coarsely broken: 3 cups
Salt: ¼ tsp.

Combine the sugar, water and vinegar in a saucepan and cook to 236°F., stirring occasionally. Remove from the heat, add the butter, nuts and salt, and beat vigorously until mixture begins to thicken. Quickly drop small amounts onto waxed paper, using two teaspoons for measuring and dropping.

Sugarplums have long been a specialty of mine and have met with great favor whenever I make them. The centers are made from the regular French Cream center fondants, and several different flavor combinations may be used.

Fruits used should be only the largest and most select. Jumbo-size, plump and meaty prunes, dried pears, dried peaches and even dried apples are excellent, while apricots are especially good when made into sugarplums. The fruit should be steamed in a colander over boiling water until it is soft and manageable before being used. Apricots and peaches may not get as soft as prunes, but they will soften enough to be manipulated, after which they will set once more. Cut prunes down the side and the pit may be extracted. Other fruits are usually stoned. They should be cut nearly in half; apricots need not be cut at all. Here are some good combinations:

FILLINGS FOR SUGARPLUMS

Milk-and-butter fondant (p. 46): 1 cup
Vanilla extract: 1 tsp.

Chopped walnuts, or walnut halves: ½ cup
Granulated sugar for coating

Mix the fondant and flavoring well. If chopped nuts are used, add them as you mix in the flavoring. With the end of a table knife, fill the fruits until they bulge with fondant, then coat fruit by rolling in granulated sugar. If desired, colored sugars may be used. If you use walnut halves, first stuff the fruit, then press a half walnut on top of the fondant, capping the fruit. Roll in sugar as directed for other combinations.

Milk-and-butter fondant: 1 cup
Oil of orange: a few drops

Chopped pecans, or pecan halves: ½ cup
Orange food color

Make up as in the preceding recipe.

Milk-and-butter fondant: 1 cup
Chopped filberts: ½ cup

Strawberry flavoring: ¼ tsp.
Red food color for light pink

Whole filberts would be impractical to use, so in this flavor, the chopped nuts are mixed into the fondant. The color should be light pink.

Milk-and-butter fondant: 1 cup   Wild cherry flavoring: a few drops
Chopped blanched almonds: ½ cup Red food color for deep pink

If desired, halves of blanched almonds may be used as caps on the fillings; in that case, no chopped nuts would be used in the fondant.

Many other combinations of nuts, candied fruits and flavors may be tried. You may either use the flavor-nut combinations as for French Creams (page 85), or live dangerously and experiment to your heart's content!

Sweet and Dandy Homemade Candy—
More Homestyle Recipes

The recipes in this section come from a folio of tested recipes from the research kitchens of the Best Foods Division of Corn Products Company. They have kindly given me permission to use them in my work and, with slight adaptations, they are presented here. I recommend that you follow the recipes as they are. You won't go wrong. I have made many of the recipes to test their practicality in my own kitchen and was very pleased with the results. Some of the recipes are duplications of the types I have given in the previous chapter of my own home recipes, but don't let that stop you from trying out both and making your selection of the one you like best. The recipes are grouped according to type and you will find that the variations suggested may be even more delectable than the basic recipe, or at least more to your liking.

CHOCOLATE FUDGE

Sugar: 3 cups
Milk: ¾ cup
Nucoa or Mazola margarine:
   3 Tbsps.
Karo corn syrup, light or dark:
   2 Tbsps.

Unsweetened chocolate:
   2 ozs.
Vanilla extract: 1 tsp.
Walnuts, coarsely chopped
   (optional): 1 cup

Combine sugar, milk, margarine, light or dark corn syrup and chocolate in heavy 3-quart saucepan. Cook over medium heat, stirring constantly, until mixture boils. Then cook, stirring occasionally, until temperature reaches 238°F. or until a small amount of mixture dropped into very cold water forms a soft ball which flattens on removal from water. Remove from heat. Add vanilla. Cool to lukewarm (110°F.). Beat until fudge begins to thicken and loses its gloss. Mix in nuts. Quickly pour into greased 8-inch square pan. Cut into squares when cold. Makes 2 pounds.

Variations:

BLOND FUDGE: Follow recipe for Chocolate Fudge, omitting chocolate and increasing corn syrup to 3 tablespoons and vanilla to 2 teaspoons.

DOUBLE DECKER FUDGE: Prepare 1 recipe Chocolate Fudge; pour into greased 9-inch square pan. Prepare 1 recipe Blond Fudge; pour over Chocolate Fudge. Cut into squares when cold. Makes 4 pounds.

EASY CREAMY FUDGE

Semi-sweet chocolate chips:
  6 ozs.
Nucoa or Mazola margarine:
  1½ Tbsps.
Karo light or dark corn syrup:
  ⅓ cup

Evaporated milk, undiluted:
  ¼ cup.
Vanilla extract: 1 tsp.
Salt: ¼ tsp.
Confectioners' sugar, sifted: 1 lb.
Chopped nuts (optional): ½ cup

Melt chocolate and margarine in double boiler top over hot water. Mix in corn syrup, undiluted evaporated milk, vanilla and salt. Add confectioners' sugar, 1 cup at a time, blending well after each addition. Stir in chopped nuts. Turn into greased 8-inch square pan. Spread quickly, to form even layer about ¾ inch thick. Cut into squares when firm. Makes about 2 pounds.

Variations:

FUDGE FROSTING: Follow recipe for Fudge, increasing evaporated milk to ¹/3 cup. Makes enough to cover tops and sides of two (8-inch) layers.

CHOCOLATE-ORANGE FROSTING: Follow recipe for Fudge Frosting, adding 1 tablespoon orange juice and 1 tablespoon grated orange rind with Karo syrup.

MOCHA FROSTING: Follow recipe for Fudge Frosting, adding 1 tablespoon instant coffee powder with Karo syrup.

FUDGE SAUCE: Follow recipe for Fudge, increasing Karo syrup and evaporated milk to ²/3 cup each. Serve hot. May be covered and stored several days in refrigerator, then reheated over hot water. Makes about 2¼ cups.

PENUCHE (PANOCHA)

Light brown sugar, firmly packed:
  3 cups*
Milk: ¾ cup
Nucoa or Mazola margarine:
  1 Tbsp.

Karo, light, dark or pancake and
  waffle corn syrup: 1 Tbsp.
Salt: ¼ tsp.
Vanilla extract: 1 tsp.
Chopped nuts (optional): 1 cup

Combine sugar, milk, Nucoa or Mazola margarine, Karo syrup and salt in saucepan. Cook over medium heat, stirring constantly, until mixture boils. Continue cooking, stirring occasionally, until temperature reaches 238°F. or until a small amount of mixture dropped into very cold water forms a soft ball which flattens on removal from water. Remove from heat. Cool to lukewarm (110°F.). Add vanilla. Beat until mixture holds its shape when dropped from spoon and loses its gloss. Quickly stir in nuts. Immediately pour into greased 8-inch square pan. Cut into squares when cool. Makes 64 one-inch squares.

*1½ cups firmly packed dark brown sugar and 1½ cups granulated sugar may be substituted for 3 cups light brown sugar.

CREAMY CARAMELS

Light cream: 2 cups
Sugar: 2 cups
Karo light or dark corn syrup:
　　1 cup

Salt: ½ tsp.
Nucoa or Mazola margarine:
　　⅓ cup
Chopped nuts: ½ cup
Vanilla extract: 1 tsp.

Heat cream to lukewarm in large heavy saucepan. Pour out 1 cup; reserve. Add sugar, corn syrup and salt to cream in saucepan. Cook over medium heat, stirring constantly, until mixture boils. Add reserved 1 cup cream very slowly, so mixture does not stop boiling. Cook 5 minutes, stirring constantly. Stir in margarine, about 1 teaspoon at a time. Turn heat to low. Boil gently, stirring constantly, until temperature reaches 248°F. or until a small amount of mixture dropped into very cold water forms a firm ball which does not flatten on removal from water. Remove from heat. Gently mix in nuts and vanilla.

Let stand 10 minutes. Stir just enough to distribute nuts. Pour into one corner of lightly greased 8-inch square pan, letting mixture flow to its own level in pan. Do *not* scrape cooking pan. Cool to room temperature. Turn out onto cutting board. (If candy sticks, heat bottom of pan slightly. Let candy cool before cutting.) Mark off ¾-inch squares. Cut with large, sharp knife. Wrap each caramel in waxed paper to store. Makes about 2 pounds.

Variations:

CREAMY CHOCOLATE CARAMELS: Follow recipe for Creamy Caramels, adding 3 to 4 ounces unsweetened chocolate with nuts and vanilla.

CREAMY RAISIN CARAMELS: Follow recipe for Creamy Caramels, adding 1 cup chopped raisins with nuts.

CARAMEL CHOCOLATE SKRUNCH

Corn flakes: 2 cups
Crisp rice cereal: 1 cup
Semi-sweet chocolate chips:
　　½ cup
Broken nuts: 1 cup

Karo dark corn syrup: ¾ cup
Sugar: ¼ cup
Nucoa or Mazola margarine:
　　2 Tbsps.
Vanilla extract: ½ tsp.

Cut both ends from a 1-quart milk carton, then set carton on waxed paper. Combine cereals, chocolate chips and nuts in large bowl; set aside. Combine corn syrup, sugar and margarine in a saucepan. Stirring constantly, bring to full boil over medium heat and boil 3 minutes. Remove from heat and cool 10 minutes. Add vanilla. Beat mixture with wooden spoon until mixture turns a light brown and thickens. Pour over cereal mixture all at once. Toss to coat evenly. Spoon out and press down firmly into milk carton. Chill until set, 1 to 2 hours. Loosen with spatula and peel off carton. It does not require refrigeration after loaf is set. Makes about 1 pound.

TO MAKE FREE-FORM SHAPES: Do not press mixture into milk carton. Cool about 15 minutes, then shape as desired, with greased hands or spoon.

BUTTERSCOTCH SKRUNCH: Follow recipe for Caramel Chocolate Skrunch, but substitute ½ cup butterscotch chips for chocolate chips.

MOCHA SKRUNCH: Follow recipe for Caramel Chocolate Skrunch, but add 1 tablespoon instant coffee powder to syrup mixture before boiling.

PEANUT AND RAISIN SKRUNCH: Follow recipe for Caramel Chocolate Skrunch, but substitute ½ cup raisins for chocolate chips, 1 cup chopped peanuts for broken nuts, and add 1 teaspoon cinnamon to syrup mixture before boiling.

PEANUT BUTTER SKRUNCH: Follow recipe for Caramel Chocolate Skrunch, but increase rice cereal to 2 cups; omit nuts and add ½ cup Skippy chunk-style peanut butter to syrup along with flavoring. If desired, almond extract may be substituted for vanilla.

SPICY CEREAL CHEWY CRUNCH

Toasted round oat cereal: 3 cups
Bite-size shredded wheat cereal:
  2 cups
Bite-size shredded rice cereal:
  2 cups
Bite-size toasted corn cereal:
  2 cups
Raisins: 1 cup
Pecan halves or walnut pieces:
  1 cup

Nucoa or Mazola margarine:
  ½ cup
Brown sugar, firmly packed:
  1⅓ cups
Karo light corn syrup: ¼ cup
Cinnamon: 2 tsps.
Salt: ½ tsp.

Toss cereal, raisins and nuts together in large greased bowl. Combine margarine, brown sugar, corn syrup, cinnamon and salt in heavy 1-quart saucepan. Stirring constantly, bring to boil over medium heat and boil 2 minutes. Pour hot syrup over mixture. Stir well to coat completely. Spread on two greased cookie sheets. When cool and firm, break into pieces. Makes about 2½ quarts.

CRUNCHY CHEWS

Karo dark corn syrup: ¾ cup
Sugar: ¾ cup
Skippy creamy or chunk-style
  peanut butter: ¾ cup

Skippy salted mixed nuts, or peanuts, broken: ¾ cup
Corn flakes: 4½ cups

Combine corn syrup and sugar in large saucepan. Bring to full boil, stirring constantly. Remove from heat. Quickly stir in peanut butter, and add mixed nuts (or peanuts) and cereal, stirring to coat evenly. Turn into greased 13½ x 9 x 2-inch pan. Cool. Cut into squares. Makes 4½ dozen 1½-inch squares.

NUTTY CHEWS

Karo light corn syrup: ½ cup
Water: ½ cup
Sugar: 2 cups

Egg white: 1
Toasted, slivered almonds:
  1 cup

Combine light corn syrup, water and sugar in heavy saucepan. Cook over medium heat, stirring constantly, until mixture comes to boil. Cook without stirring until temperature reaches

250°F. or until a small amount of mixture dropped into very cold water forms a ball which is hard enough to hold its shape, yet plastic. Just before syrup reaches 250°F. (about 246°F.) beat egg white in small bowl of electric mixer until stiff but not dry. Then beating constantly, slowly pour syrup into first mixture. Beat until mixture is very thick and satiny. Stir in nuts. Shape candy into 4 x 6 x 1½-inch loaves on waxed paper. Let stand until firm enough to cut. Makes 1¼ pounds.

PLAIN MARSHMALLOWS

Plain gelatin: 1 envelope
Cold water: ⅓ cup
Granulated sugar: ½ cup

Karo light corn syrup: ⅔ cup
Vanilla extract: ½ tsp.

Soften gelatin in cold water in a small saucepan. Place saucepan over boiling water and stir until gelatin is dissolved. Add sugar and stir until sugar is dissolved. Pour Karo syrup in a large bowl (3- to 4-quart) of electric mixer. Add vanilla, gelatin and sugar mixture to Karo syrup, and beat about 15 minutes or until mixture becomes thick and of a marshmallow consistency. Cover thoroughly bottom of 7 x 10 x 1½-inch pan with equal parts corn starch and fine granulated sugar. Pour marshmallow into pan and smooth off top with knife. Let stand in a cool place (not refrigerator) until well set, about an hour. To remove from pan, loosen around edges with a knife; invert over a board sprinkled lightly with equal parts of corn starch and fine granulated sugar. Cut into squares with a sharp knife, moistened with cold water. Roll in equal parts corn starch and fine granulated sugar. Makes about 1 pound.

Variations:

TOASTED COCONUT MARSHMALLOWS: Prepare 2 cups finely chopped toasted coconut as follows: Chop 1 package shredded coconut and place in shallow baking pan. Place in moderate oven (350°F.); stir occasionally until coconut is toasted with a delicate brown. Butter sides and bottom of pan. Sprinkle sides and bottom of pan (7 x 10 x 1½ inches) with part of coconut. Reserve balance for top and sides. Prepare Plain Marshmallows as directed above and pour into pan. Smooth off top with knife;

sprinkle top with coconut. When set remove from pan and cut as directed. Roll cut side in coconut.

CHOCOLATE MARSHMALLOWS: Follow recipe for Plain Marshmallows. When beating is half complete, gradually add, while beating, 3 tablespoons cocoa and ½ teaspoon salt. Continue beating until mixture becomes thick and of a marshmallow consistency. Proceed as directed.

FRUIT-FLAVORED MARSHMALLOWS

Fruit-flavored gelatin: 1 package
Water: ⅓ cup
Karo light corn syrup: ½ cup

Selected decorations as desired:
colored sugar, multicolored
decorators, chocolate sprinkles, tinted coconut

Sprinkle flavored gelatin chosen evenly over water in small saucepan. Let soften 5 minutes. Place over boiling water and stir until gelatin is completely dissolved. Measure Karo syrup into small mixer bowl. Pour gelatin over syrup. Beat with electric mixer at high speed until soft peaks form when beater is raised, about 5 minutes. Pour into greased 9-inch square pan. Smooth top with spatula. Let stand in cool place until set, about 1 hour. Cut into various shapes. Roll in selected decorations immediately.

Variations:
THREE-TIER MARSHMALLOWS: Prepare 3 batches of Fruit-Flavored Marshmallows, each made with a different color gelatin. As each is prepared, pour into the same greased 9-inch square pan, making three layers. Let cool as directed above. Cut into squares. Dust with combination of equal parts confectioners' sugar and Argo corn starch.

CREAMY LEMON MINTS

Sugar: 2½ cups
Water: ¾ cup
Karo light corn syrup: ½ cup
Salt: ⅛ tsp.

Egg white: 1
Lemon extract: ¼ tsp.
Yellow food coloring

Combine sugar, water, Karo syrup and salt in heavy saucepan. Cook over medium heat, stirring constantly, until sugar is dissolved and mixture comes to boil. Continue cooking, without stirring, until temperature reaches 240°F. or until a small amount of mixture dropped into very cold water forms a soft ball that flattens on removal from water. Meanwhile, beat egg white until stiff peaks form when beater is raised. Beating constantly, gradually pour hot syrup mixture over beaten egg white; continue beating until mixture is well blended and thick. Add lemon extract and coloring. Beat with spoon until mixture is very thick and loses its gloss. Drop by tablespoonfuls on waxed paper lightly dusted with confectioners' sugar. Shape each mound into roll ½ inch thick. Cut into small pieces. Cover lightly with waxed paper. Let stand several hours or overnight to set. Store in covered container. Makes about 1¼ pounds.

PARTY MINTS

Egg whites: 3　　　　　　　　**Peppermint extract: 1 tsp.**
Karo light corn syrup: 1 Tbsp.　**Food coloring, if desired**
Confectioners' sugar, sifted: 9 cups

Beat egg whites until foamy. Add corn syrup and beat until stiff, but not dry, and peaks form when beaters are raised. Gradually add confectioners' sugar, beating well with wooden spoon after each addition. Add flavoring and, if desired, food coloring after the first addition of sugar. Continue to add sugar until mixture holds shape (mixture will be very stiff) but is not sticky to the touch. Continue blending by kneading with hands until smooth.

Divide mixture into thirds. Between two pieces of waxed paper, roll out each third to ¼- to ⅛-inch thickness. Refrigerate one hour. Remove top layer of waxed paper. Cut in desired shapes.* Decorate with leaves and flowers, using a colored confectioners' sugar frosting or a commercial cake decorator. To harden, leave uncovered at room temperature several hours before serving. Mints can be stored in covered container. Makes about 11 dozen 1¼-inch circles.

*To cut shapes, use 1¼-inch biscuit cutter, center of doughnut cutter or miniature aspic or jelly cutters.

Variation:

CALLA LILY: Fold each cut 1¼-inch circle in half. Pinch one end of semi-circle together; separate other end by folding back the upper edge slightly. Decorate with 2 yellow sugar icing dots inside fold and put a green leaf at base where pinched together.

MINTED WALNUTS

Sugar: 1 cup
Water: ½ cup
Karo light corn syrup: ¼ cup
Marshmallows: 10 regular

Essence of peppermint: 1 tsp.
Food coloring (optional): 10 drops
Walnut halves: 3 cups

Combine sugar, water and corn syrup in heavy 2-quart saucepan. Cook over medium heat, stirring constantly, until mixture boils. Continue cooking to 238°F. or until a small amount of mixture dropped into very cold water forms a soft ball which flattens on removal from water. Remove from heat. Quickly add marshmallows and essence of peppermint. Stir until marshmallows are completely melted. Stir in food coloring, if desired. Add walnut halves and stir until well coated. Pour on waxed paper. Separate halves while still warm. Makes 1¼ pounds.

NOTE: Recipe may also be prepared substituting 3 cups pecan halves, or 3½ cups peanuts, or 3½ cups almonds for walnut halves.

Variation:

ORANGE-FLAVORED WALNUTS: Follow recipe for Minted Walnuts, but substitute ½ teaspoon orange extract for essence of peppermint.

QUICK COOK FONDANT

Nucoa or Mazola margarine:
   ⅓ cup
Karo light corn syrup: ½ cup

Confectioners' sugar, sifted: 1 lb.
Vanilla extract: 1 tsp.

Combine margarine, corn syrup and half the sugar in a 3-quart saucepan. Cook over low heat, stirring constantly, until mixture comes to full boil. Quickly stir in remaining sugar and vanilla. Remove from heat immediately. Stir just until mixture holds its shape. Pour into greased pan. Cool just enough to handle and knead until smooth. Knead in any desired flavoring and coloring and shape as desired with lightly-greased hands. (If candy hardens too much before kneading, work with a spoon, then knead.)

Variations:

MINT PATTIES: Flavor fondant peppermint or wintergreen and tint red or green. Shape into patties.

BONBONS: Flavor and tint fondant as desired. Shape into balls with nut pieces in center. Roll in colored or white sugar or in chocolate or multicolor sprinkles for decorating.

FILLED FRUITS OR NUTS: Fill center of pitted prunes, dates or apricots with fondant or place fondant between nut halves. Roll in sugar.

EASTER EGGS: Flavor fondant as desired. Tint pastel color(s). Shape like eggs. Decorate with thin confectioners' sugar icing, tinted if desired. Put into nests of colored coconut. (Color coconut by tossing with few drops food coloring.)

POPCORN TREE: Prepare 14 cups popped corn. Line 13 x 9 x 2-inch pan with aluminum foil, letting foil extend over sides of pan. Cook Fondant as directed but substitute 2 tablespoons water for the 1/3 cup margarine, and increase light corn syrup to 1 cup. Stir in sugar remaining (omit vanilla). Remove from heat as soon as all sugar is added, and stir in 32 regular-size marshmallows and 1 teaspoon peppermint flavoring. Pour over popped corn in large bowl. Toss until popped corn is well coated. Press into prepared pan. Cool until set, about 15 minutes. Remove from pan and foil. Cut into pieces as follows: two *each* about 5 x 5 inches, 4 x 4 inches and 2 x 2 inches; three about 3 x 3 inches. Stack pieces, largest on bottom, smallest on top, centering alternating corners over sides. Support with dowel stick through center if needed. Decorate with green sugar, small candies and birthday candles.

POPCORN BALLS: Prepare popcorn mixture as directed for Popcorn Tree. Shape into 2½-inch balls, pressing lightly but firmly. Grease hands with margarine for ease in handling. Makes 16.

CHOCOLATE FONDANT: Sift ¼ cup cocoa with 1 pound confectioners' sugar. Follow recipe for Quick Cook Fondant, using cocoa mixture instead of plain confectioners' sugar.

"NO-COOK" FONDANT

Nucoa or Mazola margarine: ⅓ cup
Karo light corn syrup: ⅓ cup
Vanilla extract: 1 tsp.
Salt: 1 tsp.
Confectioners' sugar, sifted: 1 lb.

Blend margarine, light corn syrup, vanilla and salt in large mixing bowl. Add confectioners' sugar all at once and mix in, first with spoon, then kneading with hands. Turn out onto board and continue kneading until mixture is well blended and smooth. Store in cool place in a covered bowl. When ready to use, shape as desired. Makes 1¹/3 pounds.

Variations:
MINT PATTIES: Follow recipe for No-Cook Fondant, substituting 1 teaspoon peppermint or wintergreen flavoring for vanilla. Tint desired color, using red or green food coloring. Shape into balls or roll thin and cut into desired shapes.

ORANGE OR LEMON CREAMS: Follow recipe for No-Cook Fondant, substituting 2 teaspoons orange extract or 1 teaspoon lemon extract for vanilla. Tint delicate orange or yellow with food coloring. Shape as directed for Mint Patties.

PEANUT SQUARES: Follow recipe for No-Cook Fondant, mixing in ¾ cup coarsely chopped unsalted peanuts. Roll out or pat to ½-inch thickness. Cut into squares.

ALMOND DIAMONDS: Follow recipe for No-Cook Fondant, substituting 1 teaspoon almond extract for vanilla. Mix in ½ cup coarsely chopped, toasted, blanched almonds. Roll out or pat to ½-inch thickness. Cut into diamonds.

CANDIED FRUIT SQUARES: Follow recipe for No-Cook Fondant, substituting rum or rum flavoring for vanilla, if desired. Mix in ½ cup finely chopped mixed candied fruit. Roll out to ½-inch thickness. Cut squares.

MOCHA LOGS: Follow recipe for No-Cook Fondant, adding 2 teaspoons instant coffee powder. Shape into rolls, about 2 inches long and ½ inch thick. Roll in chocolate sprinkles.

CIRCUS BALLS: Shape No-Cook Fondant into ½-inch balls. Roll in multicolored decorators.

NUT CREAMS: Shape No-Cook Fondant into ½-inch balls. Press between two walnut or pecan halves.

STUFFED DATES: Shape No-Cook Fondant into very small finger-shaped rolls and stuff into pitted dates. Roll in granulated sugar. Recipe makes enough fondant to stuff about 1¾ pounds dates.

CHOCOLATE PATTIES: Follow recipe for No-Cook Fondant, adding ¼ cup cocoa to confectioners' sugar before sifting. Shape fondant into balls or roll thin and cut into desired shapes.

MARZIPAN CANDY

Karo light corn syrup: 3 Tbsps.
Vanilla extract: ¼ tsp.
Almond extract: ¼ tsp.
Salt: dash

Milk: 1 Tbsp.
Confectioners' sugar, sifted:
  1½ cups
Almond paste*: 1 cup

Combine light corn syrup, vanilla, almond extract and salt. Blend in milk. Add confectioners' sugar; mix well. Blend with almond paste. Shape mixture as desired.** Let stand uncovered, to dry thoroughly. Makes about ¾ pound.

---

*May be bought in cans at specialty food or confectioners' supply shops.
**AUTHOR'S NOTE: Marzipan can be shaped like miniature fruit, colored with diluted food coloring applied with a clean camels' hair brush. Other shapes are also possible, and these make gay colorful party or gift candies.

OLD-FASHIONED EASTER EGGS

Fondant*: 1 recipe
Peanut Butter Coconut Centers
  (below): 1 recipe

Chocolate Chews (below):
  1 recipe
Confectioners' sugar frosting

Flatten each piece of fondant to ¼-inch thickness with hands. Wrap half the number of pieces around Peanut Butter Coconut Centers and the other half around Chocolate Chews. Form each into egg shape. Decorate with confectioners' sugar frosting piped through decorating tube. Serve leftover centers and chews as candies. Makes 10 large or 36 small decorated eggs (half with Peanut Butter Coconut Centers and half with Chocolate Chews), plus 5 large or 18 small candies of each type.

NO-COOK PEANUT BUTTER COCONUT CENTERS

Skippy creamy or chunk-style
  peanut butter: ¼ cup
Karo dark corn syrup: ¼ cup
Water: 2 tsps.
Flaked coconut: 1 can (3½ ozs.)

Confectioners' sugar, sifted:
  1²/₃ cups
Nonfat dry milk (dry form):
  3 Tbsps.
Salt: ¼ tsp.

Blend Skippy peanut butter and corn syrup. Stir in water. Combine confectioners' sugar, nonfat dry milk and salt. Stir into syrup mixture. Add coconut. Knead until thoroughly blended. Shape into 10 large or 36 small balls.

NO-COOK CHOCOLATE CHEWS

Nucoa or Mazola margarine:
  1 Tbsp.
Karo syrup, light or dark: ¼ cup
Unsweetened chocolate, melted:
  1 oz.

Vanilla extract: ½ tsp.
Confectioners' sugar, sifted:
  1½ cups
Nonfat dry milk (dry form):
  ¹/₃ cup

Blend margarine and corn syrup. Stir in chocolate and vanilla. Combine confectioners' sugar and nonfat dry milk. Gradually

*See No-Cook Fondant (p. 148) or use 6 cups Basic Fondant Recipe (p. 46).

add to syrup mixture. Stir, then knead until thoroughly blended. Shape into 10 large or 36 small balls.

PEANUT BRITTLE

Karo syrup, light or dark: 1 cup
Sugar: 1 cup
Water: ¼ cup

Nucoa or Mazola margarine:
   2 Tbsps.
Skippy salted peanuts: 1½ cups
Baking soda: 1 tsp.

Combine corn syrup, sugar, water and margarine in heavy 2-quart saucepan. Cook over medium heat, stirring constantly until sugar is dissolved and mixture comes to boil. Continue cooking without stirring until temperature reaches 280°F. or until a small amount of mixture dropped into very cold water separates into threads that are hard but not brittle. Gradually stir in salted peanuts as mixture continues to boil. Cook, stirring frequently, until temperature reaches 300°F. or until small amount of mixture dropped into very cold water separates into threads that are hard and brittle. Remove from heat. Add baking soda; blend quickly, but thoroughly. Immediately turn onto heavily greased baking or cookie sheet. Spread mixture evenly to edges of baking sheet with a greased metal spatula. When cool, break into pieces. Makes 1½ pounds.

OLD-FASHIONED BUTTERSCOTCH

Brown sugar, firmly packed:
   2 cups
Karo dark corn syrup: ¼ cup
New Nucoa or Mazola margarine:
   ¼ cup

Water: 2 Tbsps.
Vinegar: 2 Tbsps.

Combine all ingredients in 3-quart saucepan. Bring to boil, stirring constantly. Cook over medium heat, stirring occasionally, until mixture reaches 300°F. or until a small amount of mixture dropped into very cold water separates into threads that are hard and brittle. Pour into greased pans. Mark into squares as candy hardens. Makes 1 pound.

PRALINES I

Granulated sugar: 2 cups
Milk: ^{2}/$_3$ cup
Karo dark, or pancake and waffle
   corn syrup: ^{1}/$_3$ cup

Salt: ^{1}/$_4$ tsp.
Vanilla extract: ^{1}/$_2$ tsp.
Pecan meats: 1 cup

Combine first four ingredients in saucepan. Cook over medium heat, stirring constantly, until sugar is dissolved. Cook without stirring, to soft-ball stage (238°F.) or until a small amount of mixture forms a soft ball when tested in very cold water. Remove from heat and cool to lukewarm (110°F.). Add vanilla. Then beat until mixture is thick and creamy. Stir in pecans. Drop from tip of spoon onto waxed paper. Shape with a spoon to form a circle and to spread pecans so that they are only one layer deep. Allow to remain undisturbed until the pralines are firm and sugared. Makes 1¼ pounds.

Variation:
VANILLA PRALINES: Follow recipe for Pralines. Substitute Karo light corn syrup for dark syrup. Increase vanilla to 1 teaspoon.

PRALINES II

Light brown sugar: 1 lb.
Evaporated milk: 1 can (5^1/$_3$ ozs.)
Karo light corn syrup: 2 Tbsps.

Nucoa or Mazola margarine:
   ¼ cup
Vanilla extract: 1 tsp.
Pecan halves: 1½ cups

Combine sugar, evaporated milk and corn syrup in 2-quart saucepan. Cook over medium heat, stirring constantly, until mixture comes to a boil. Continue cooking, stirring occasionally, until temperature reaches 238°F. or until a small amount of mixture forms a soft ball when tested in very cold water. Remove from heat and add margarine. Do not stir. Cool to lukewarm (110°F.). Add vanilla and beat until creamy, then stir in pecans. Drop by teaspoonfuls on waxed paper. Shape with a spoon into a 2½-inch circle, spreading pecans as evenly as possible. Allow to remain undisturbed until the pralines are firm and sugared. Makes 1½ pounds.

BUTTERSCOTCH PECAN PRALINES

Sugar: 1 cup
Brown sugar, firmly packed: ½ cup
Evaporated milk, undiluted: ½ cup
Karo light corn syrup: ⅓ cup

Salt: dash
Nucoa or Mazola margarine:
   ⅓ cup
Vanilla extract: 1 tsp.
Pecans, coarsely chopped: 1 cup

Combine sugars, evaporated milk, corn syrup and salt in sauce-pan. Cook over medium heat, stirring constantly, until sugar is dissolved and mixture boils. Cook without stirring until mixture reaches 238°F. or until a small amount dropped into very cold water forms a soft ball which flattens on removal from water. Remove from heat. Add margarine and vanilla. Cool to lukewarm (110°F.). Beat until thick and creamy. Stir in nuts. Drop by teaspoonfuls on waxed paper. Let stand overnight. Makes 2 dozen.

SALTWATER TAFFY

Sugar: 1 cup
Argo corn starch: 2 Tbsps.
Karo light corn syrup: ¾ cup
Water: ½ cup

Salt: ½ tsp.
Nucoa or Mazola margarine:
   2 Tbsps.
Vanilla extract: 2 tsps.

Combine sugar and corn starch in saucepan. Stir in light corn syrup, water and salt. Add margarine. Cook over medium heat, stirring constantly, until mixture boils and sugar is completely dissolved. Continue cooking, without stirring, until temperature reaches 260°F. or until a small amount of mixture dropped into very cold water forms a ball which is hard enough to hold its shape, yet plastic. Remove from heat. Stir in vanilla. Pour into well-greased 9-inch square pan. Let stand until cool enough to handle. Pull until taffy has satin-like finish and light color. Pull into long strips, ½ inch wide. Cut into 1-inch pieces with scissors. Wrap pieces individually in waxed paper. Makes about 1 pound.

Variations:
PEPPERMINT TAFFY: Follow recipe for Saltwater Taffy, substitut-

ing peppermint extract for vanilla and adding 1 small drop green food coloring with extract.

BROWN SUGAR TAFFY: Follow recipe for Saltwater Taffy, substituting firmly packed brown sugar for granulated sugar and dark corn syrup for light corn syrup.

CANDY APPLES

Medium red apples: 8
Flat wooden skewers or spoons: 8
Sugar: 2 cups
Karo light corn syrup: 1 cup

Water: ½ cup
Red cinnamon candies: ¼ cup
(one 1¾-oz. bottle)
Red food coloring (optional): 10 drops

Wash and dry apples; remove stems and insert skewers into stem ends. Combine sugar, light corn syrup and water in heavy 2-quart saucepan. Stirring constantly, cook over medium heat until mixture boils and sugar is dissolved. Then cook, without stirring, until temperature reaches 250°F. or until small amount of syrup dropped into very cold water forms ball which is hard enough to hold its shape, yet is plastic. Add cinnamon candies and continue cooking to 285°F. or until small amount of syrup dropped into very cold water separates into threads which are hard, but not brittle. Remove from heat. Stir in red food coloring, if desired. Hold each apple by its skewer and quickly twirl in syrup, tilting pan to coat apple with syrup. Remove apple from syrup; allow excess to drip off, then twirl to spread syrup smoothly over apple. Place on lightly greased baking sheet to cool. Store in cool place. Makes 8.

NOTE: If candy mixture cools too quickly it may be reheated over low heat.

Variations:

CRUNCHY CANDY APPLES: Follow recipe for Candy Apples, but after coating, roll bottom quarter of apples in slightly crushed corn flakes before placing on buttered baking sheet to cool.

CANDY APPLE FACES: Prepare Candy Apples. Pour small amount of Karo light corn syrup into small bowl; let stand until sticky.

For hair, dip end of apple into syrup, then into flaked coconut. Dip round peppermint candies or small gumdrops into light corn syrup and stick on apple for eyes, nose and mouth.

CINNAMON CANDY APPLES: Increase sugar to 3 cups and reduce light corn syrup to ½ cup. Omit cinnamon candies. Cook as above until candy mixture temperature reaches 285°F. or until a small amount of syrup dropped into very cold water separates into threads which are hard, but not brittle. Remove from heat. Add 1 drop oil of cinnamon and 1 teaspoon red food coloring. Stir just enough to mix. Continue as for Candy Apples.

QUICK CANDIED POPCORN MIXTURE

Mazola corn oil: ¼ cup
Popcorn (unpopped): ½ cup
Karo light or dark corn syrup:
  ⅔ cup

Sugar: ⅔ cup
Salt: ½ tsp.

Heat corn oil in 4-quart kettle over medium heat 3 minutes. Add popcorn. Cover, leaving small air space at edge. Shake frequently over medium heat until popping stops. Mix syrup, sugar and salt in heavy saucepan. Cook over medium heat, stirring constantly, until sugar and salt are dissolved, about 2 minutes. Flavor with essence of peppermint or wintergreen, if desired. Add popped corn and stir over medium heat until corn is evenly and completely coated with syrup mixture, 3 to 5 minutes. Remove from heat. Use in one or more of the following ways:

Variations:
POPCORN BALLS: Form popcorn into balls, using as little pressure as possible. Insert wooden stick into balls, if desired. Makes six 2½-inch balls.

POPCORN WREATHS: Shape popcorn on waxed paper, making wreaths 5 to 6 inches in diameter for hanging and about 9 inches in diameter for centerpiece. Decorate with holly leaves cut from preserved angelica, small red cinnamon candies and silver dragées. Makes 2 small or 1 large wreath.

POPCORN CANDLE: Cut top off ½-pint cream carton. Wash and dry carton. Pack with popcorn. Insert small candy cane into top for wick. Peel off carton when popcorn is cool and set.

NOTES: *Do not double* popcorn recipe

Use margarine on hands when forming balls, etc.

If popcorn mixture cools during shaping and does not stick together, place over low heat a few minutes

When using Karo light corn syrup, mixture may be tinted with food coloring as desired before adding the popped corn.

QUICK BUTTERSCOTCH POPCORN

Butterscotch chips*:
  1 package (6 ozs.)

Karo light or dark corn syrup:
  ½ cup
Popped corn: 5 cups

Combine butterscotch chips and corn syrup in double boiler top. Heat over boiling water until butterscotch chips are completely melted. Stir to blend well. Pour over popped corn. Stir until well coated. Spread in lightly greased 9 x 9 x 2-inch pan; cool and cut into squares. Makes sixteen 2¼-inch squares.

CARAMEL POPCORN

Mazola corn oil: ¼ cup
Popcorn (unpopped): ½ cup
Skippy salted peanuts (or cashew nuts): 1 cup
Karo dark corn syrup: 1 cup

Sugar: 1 cup
Water: ¼ cup
Nucoa or Mazola margarine:
  ¼ cup

Heat oil in a 4-quart kettle over medium heat for 3 minutes. Add popcorn. Cover, leaving small air space at edge of cover. Shake frequently over medium heat until popping stops. Put popcorn into large greased heat-resistant bowl. Add nuts. Place mixture in preheated slow oven (300°F.) until syrup is prepared.

Combine dark corn syrup, sugar, water and margarine in a heavy 2-quart saucepan. Stirring constantly, bring to boil over medium heat. Continue cooking, stirring occasionally, until temperature reaches 280°F. or until small amount of syrup

*Or use Old-Fashioned Butterscotch (p. 151) or Butterscotch (p. 132).

dropped into very cold water separates into threads that are hard but not brittle.

Remove popcorn mixture from oven. Gradually pour syrup over mixture, stirring quickly to make sure that kernels are evenly coated. Spread mixture on two greased baking sheets. Spread out into thin layer with hands greased with margarine. Cool. Separate into clusters. Makes about 1½ pounds. Store in tightly covered container.

Part Three

Special candies
for
problem diets

Non-allergenic Candies

A large number of people today are allergic to something. Many are allergic to chocolate and for that reason are denied the pleasure of eating this most enjoyable substance. Granted that the texture and color of chocolate are very great contributing factors to its enjoyment, those people who cannot ingest chocolate without dire results may still enjoy (at least in part) the flavor of this delectable tropical bean.

Carob powder—or St. John's Bread powder, as it is sometimes called, for what reason I cannot discover—is a product made from the long pods of the carob tree, originally found only in the Mediterranean region. It is related to the jacaranda tree of South America. Carob pods contain a sweetish pulp that is dried and powdered. Also of interest is the fact that the seeds of the carob tree are so uniform in size and so constant in their weight that they were used for many years as a standard of weight in the gem and jewelry trades. It is from the tree's name that we derive our word for a measure of weight—carat.

Carob powder imparts a flavor to recipes that is surprisingly like that of chocolate, and for this reason it is extensively used in candy- and cake-making to replace the genuine product. Recipes using carob powder have been supplied me by several persons, and I pass them on here for your use.

From Mrs. Mildred Arthur, of Glen Rock, New Jersey, come the following:

MILDRED ARTHUR'S FUDGE-TYPE CANDY

Carob powder: 1/3 cup
Powdered skim milk solids:
  2/3 cup
Butter or margarine: 1/4 cup

Honey: 1/4 cup
Vanilla extract: 1 tsp.
Pecans, chopped or whole:
  1/2 cup

Blend all together well, then spread on waxed paper laid on a cookie sheet. Refrigerate until chilled, then cut into squares. Keep refrigerated in summer, because of the butter. No refrigeration is needed if margarine is used.

VARIATION I, FUDGE-TYPE CANDY

Carob powder: 1/4 cup
Powdered skim milk solids:
  1/2 cup

Honey: 3 Tbsps. (or less,
  to make stiff paste)

Blend all together, form into small balls and roll in finely shredded coconut, chopped nuts or wheat germ.

VARIATION II, FUDGE-TYPE CANDY

Carob powder: 1/4 cup
Powdered skim milk solids:
  1/2 cup

Honey: 3 Tbsps. (or less,
  to make a stiff paste)
Shredded wheat, well-rolled:
  1/2 cup

Blend all together well, form into small balls and roll in coatings, as above.

MILDRED ARTHUR'S SUNNY PEPS

Smooth or chunky peanut butter:
  1/2 cup
Honey: 1/2 cup
Powdered skim milk solids:
  3/4 cup

Wheat germ (optional):
  1/2 cup
Raisins: 1/3 cup
Shelled sunflower seeds:
  1/3 cup

Blend all together thoroughly, form into small balls; then roll in sesame seeds, ground nuts, finely shredded coconut or wheat germ. If optional wheat germ is used in the recipe, *do not* roll in sesame seeds. The blend of the two is not a good one.

VARIATION OF SUNNY PEPS

Peanut butter: ½ cup
Honey: ½ cup
Powdered skim milk solids:
  1 cup

Raisins (try white ones):
  ½ cup
Chopped peanuts: ½ cup

Blend all ingredients, then place on waxed paper on a cookie sheet and refrigerate to set. Cut into squares when set.

Barth Vitamin Corporation (page 9) has also supplied me with a few recipes using health food ingredients, including carob. Barth's is a mail-order house, dealing with all kinds of health foods, vitamin foods and similar items. They provide a catalog upon request. The company also manufactures certain compounds which can be used in candymaking recipes: Car-O-Bar, Kayno and powdered whey for instance. These ingredients appear in some of the adapted recipes presented here.

CAROB HEALTH CANDY

Rose hips powder: 1 Tbsp.
Food yeast: 1 Tbsp.
Bone meal: 1 Tbsp.
Lecithin granules: 1 Tbsp.

Nut butter (peanut or cashew):
  2 Tbsps.
Melted Car-O-Bar: 2 Tbsps.
Kayno: 2 Tbsps.

Blend all ingredients together and form into small balls. Roll balls in sesame seeds or sunflower seed meal, pressing the balls between the palms of your hands to make the seeds stick to the outside. These make excellent snacks for the children.

CAROB POWDER FUDGE

Carob powder: 6 Tsbps.
Raw sugar: 2 cups
Milk: ²/₃ cup
Sesame seeds, lightly toasted:
  ½ cup

Vanilla extract: 1½ tsps.
Shelled sunflower seeds:
  ½ cup
Sunflower seed oil: 2 Tbsps.

Combine carob powder with the raw sugar and mix; add the milk and cook to 230°F. Remove from heat. Add sunflower seed oil, vanilla and seeds. Beat until creamy, pour into well-oiled pan and, when set, cut into 1½-inch squares.

SUNFLOWER CAR-O-BAR CLUSTERS

Melted Car-O-Bar: 2 ozs.
Sunflower seed oil: ¹/₃ cup
Beaten egg: 1
Whole shelled sunflower seeds:
  1 cup
Vanilla extract: 1 tsp.

Kayno (or raw sugar):
  ½ cup
Whole grain pastry flour:
  ½ cup
Sea salt (or Kosher salt):
  1 pinch

Heat the Car-O-Bar with the oil until melted, then cool. Add the beaten egg, sunflower seeds and vanilla to the cooled Car-O-Bar oil mixture; blend well. Sift the sugar, flour and salt together, then blend into the carob mixture. Drop from teaspoon on a greased cookie sheet. Bake for 8 minutes at 350°F. Remove from the sheet while hot, being careful not to break them, for they are fragile. This recipe makes a chewy, candy-like cookie.

CAROB KISSES

Sesame seeds: ½ cup
Kayno (or raw sugar): 1½ cups
Honey: ¹/₃ cup

Powdered whey: ¹/₃ cup
Carob powder: ¹/₃ cup
Butter or margarine: 1 Tbsp.

Butter a shallow pan and spread sesame seeds in an even layer on the bottom. Combine all other ingredients in a saucepan and cook until the temperature reaches 250°F. Remove from heat and pour the cooked candy over the seeds; let stand until cold.

Form into small balls and roll each into a twist of waxed paper, in the manner of old-fashioned candy kisses. Whole sunflower seeds, shelled, may be substituted for sesame seeds or the two may be mixed. Salted shelled sunflower seeds are also good substitutes for sesame seeds.

Low-Calorie Candies

While I told you in the first chapter that candy, eaten as it should be—and not to excess, is no more fattening than many other foods that you eat, there will be some people who cannot bring themselves to accept this fact (or to discipline themselves) and who are therefore afraid to indulge themselves now and then unless the caloric content of candy is greatly reduced. This is, of course, why stores sell tons of "low-cal" foods and drinks. Some people, too, may be under orders by their doctors to limit their caloric intake.

To this group of "Twiggys" I offer a few recipes made from natural or health food ingredients that are lower in calories than, for instance, a rich chocolate cream, but satisfy the craving for something delicious that tastes sweet. Most of these ingredients can be found in supermarkets. Those that are not obtainable there will be available at health food stores. I detest the appellation "health food," for it implies in some roundabout way that all the other things we eat are *not* healthy for us. Natural foods would be a better name for the many items sold in these establishments, because most of them are left in as natural a condition as possible until cooked or consumed, without processing to remove hulls, skins or other parts and without loss of nutritional content.

Some things found in these stores may make the uninitiated dive for the nearest bottle of digestive tablets. Others are surprisingly tasty and a few are outright delicious. In any case we can combine some of these items in candy recipes and eat them with a clear conscience, so far as weight control is concerned.

POWDERED CITRUS PEELS

Two ingredients I have not been able to find—even in health food stores—are powdered grapefruit and lime. The Spice Islands line, a product of Leslie Foods, Inc., San Francisco, California, however, offers powdered orange and lemon peels that are excellent for our use.

To make your own powdered grapefruit and lime peels, select perfect fruit and before cutting it, scrub the rind furiously with a brush, hot water and a little soap. Rinse with a brush and hot water to remove soap. This drastic treatment is to remove all possible additives and sprays from fruits sold in the stores, not the least of which are any of a dozen pesticides, also a coating of wax applied to keep the surface looking fresh and ripe even when the fruit is something less that prime. So much for commercial ethics.

After cleaning the fruit, pare off the upper rind in thin strips. Take as little of the pithy white inner rind as possible. Do not squeeze the strips as you pare them any more than necessary as the oil within them is the flavoring medium, and this you should retain. Spread the strips on a cookie sheet or in a shallow tray and keep in a warm place to dry. In full sun is fine, provided you lay one thickness of cheesecloth over the peel to ward off insect invaders.

When the peel is completely dry—this means "snapping" dry (when you pick up a piece and stress it, it should snap easily in two)—grind them into a fine powder. Use a blender or crush the peels with a rolling pin, or pound them in a large mortar or mash with the bowl of a heavy tablespoon in small bowl. The grindings should be sifted often as you work so as to size the particles uniformly. Put back the large ones for another grinding.

The completed powder will keep for some time in tightly closed jars.

LEMON FRUIT LOGS

Figs: 1 cup
Pitted dates: 1 cup
White raisins: 1 cup

Chopped pecans: 1½ cups
Lemon juice: 2 Tbsps.
Powdered lemon rind: ½ cup

Mix the fruit together, then pass all through a food grinder. Into the resulting paste, mix thoroughly the nuts, lemon juice and powdered lemon rind. Shape into small rolls and roll in lightly toasted sesame seeds.

ORANGE FRUIT LOGS

Substitute fresh orange juice and powdered orange rind for the lemon ingredients in the above recipe, and use chopped walnuts in place of the pecans. Otherwise proceed as in Lemon Fruit Logs recipe.

GRAPEFRUIT FRUIT LOGS

Substitute fresh grapefruit juice and rind, and use chopped filberts. Roll the logs in chopped sunflower seeds instead of sesame seeds.

LIME FRUIT LOGS

Substitute fresh lime juice and rind, and use chopped almonds. Blanch the almonds before chopping them. Roll the logs in wheat germ.

SUNFLOWER ROLL

Milk: 1 cup
Honey: 1½ cups
Chopped, pitted dates: 1 cup
Chopped pecans: ½ cup

Chopped dried fruit* (peaches,
    pears, apples or apricots):
    ½ cup
Soy-bean grits: ¼ cup

*The fruit can be mixed if desired.

Bring the milk to a boil, stir in the honey then add the fruit and cook, stirring constantly, to 240°F. Remove from heat and let stand until cool, then mix in the nuts and soy grits. Beat the mixture until stiff, then roll out into a thick log. Roll the log in chopped sunflower seeds. When firm enough, cut into ½-inch thick slices.

DIET SUGARPLUMS

Large dried prunes, pitted: 1 lb.
Chopped, pitted dates: 1 cup
White raisins: ½ cup

Nuts, chopped: ⅓ cup
Sesame seeds, lightly toasted: ¼ cup
Shelled sunflower seeds: ¼ cup

Steam the prunes slightly in a colander over boiling water to soften them. Grind the dates and raisins together in a food grinder, then add the nuts and seeds and mix thoroughly. Stuff the prunes with this mixture. To coat, roll in raw sugar and chopped, shredded coconut or in wheat germ.

Sugarplums are sure to be a great success with all your friends.

SESAME BALLS

Light cream: 1/3 cup
Honey: 2/3 cup
Molasses: 1/3 cup

Sunflower seed oil: 1 Tbsp.
Soy-bean grits: 1/4 cup
Sesame seeds, lightly toasted:
    1 cup

Place the cream, honey, molasses and oil in a pan and cook to 235°F. Remove from heat and add the grits and sesame seeds, then beat until thick. Drop from teaspoon on a greased cookie sheet and chill in the refrigerator. Roll into balls after the candy is cold. Keep refrigerated until time to serve.

CREAM CHEESE NUTTIES

Philadelphia cream cheese:
    1 cup
Salt: 1/8 tsp.
Honey: 2 Tbsps.

Chopped pecans: 1/4 cup
Chopped shredded coconut:
    1/2 cup
Powdered orange rind: 2 Tbsps.

Mix all ingredients and form into small balls. If preferred, the balls can be rolled in wheat germ or in lightly toasted sesame seeds.

HONEY "MARSHMALLOWS"

Unflavored gelatin: 2 envelopes
Fresh coconut juice: 1/4 cup

Honey: 1 cup
Shredded *fresh* coconut:
    3 cups

Soften the gelatin in the coconut juice. Bring the honey to a boil, then place in large bowl of mixer and start to beat. Add the softened gelatin slowly to the honey and beat until very light —not less than 10 to 15 minutes. Pour into oiled 9-inch square cake pans and let stand for two days to set.

Turn out of pans and cut into squares, then roll the squares in the shredded coconut. If the candy sticks to the knife when cutting, wet the blade in cold water.

If the top surface dries so much that the coconut will not stick to it, the surface may be wiped with a cloth dampened with very hot water, and then the coconut may be sprinkled over it. The candy can then be cut and rolled in the remaining coconut. An alternate method would be to spread a layer of coconut on the top of the candy immediately after it is first poured into the pans; or, a layer can be put into the pan and the candy poured on top, then additional coconut sprinkled on the top. This method will leave only the freshly cut sides of the squares to be covered with shredded coconut.

High-Altitude Candymaking

Often people living in mountain areas cannot seem to make a cookbook recipe come out right, and they do not know the cause of the failure. The reason is really very simple, as is the cure. Liquids boil at different temperatures, according to the different altitudes.

The bald statement that water boils at 212°F. is true only at sea level. In Denver, Colorado—the Mile-High City—water boils at a lower temperature: approximately 202°F. How can you figure out how to adjust the temperatures called for in recipes? If you do not already know the altitude of your home town, your local weather station, radio station or school science department should be able to tell you. Simply deduct from the temperature required by the recipe two degrees for every thousand feet of altitude above sea level, if you know the altitude. If not, there is another way. Even without knowing the altitude, you can adjust the recipes in this book to your location by a simple calculation. You don't have to be a mathematician to do it, either.

Choose any recipe in this book; for example, the Lollipop recipe that calls for the candy to be cooked to 300°F. This is, of course, at sea level. Subtract the sea level boiling point for water from this—212°—and the answer is 88°. This is the amount *above the boiling point* called for by the recipe. Now bring a pan of water to a boil, a *full* boil. Hold your accurate candy thermometer in the water so that the bulb does not touch the pan but is completely submerged. Read the temperature carefully and write it in this book as a permanent record. Let us assume that the water boiled for you at 202°F. Add to this figure the 88° obtained by the above subtraction and you will obtain the temperature for cooking the lollipops: 290°F. instead of the recipe's 300°. The boiling point of 202°F. will also tell you that you live at about 5000 feet above sea level (or two degrees for every thousand feet of altitude). Having worked this out, you are now an amateur physicist as well as a candymaker!

In future, these calculations may be applied to any recipe that calls for boiling. Simply subtract 212° from the temperature indicated in the recipe, and then add the difference obtained to the boiling point figure at your location.

A word about thermometers might not be amiss at this point. Most thermometers used in cooking and candymaking will not be perfectly accurate at high altitudes. They have been calibrated to operate at sea level and may prove inaccurate or even erratic at higher altitudes. The difference between "inaccurate" and "erratic" is an important one. If the thermometer is inaccurate, it merely means that it will register incorrectly and will do so consistently. If the instrument is erratic, however, it means that one time it will register an inaccurate temperature and the next time another (but different) temperature, that is also inaccurate. Needless to say, such a thermometer cannot be used with any degree of confidence in candymaking.

For this reason, especially if you live in a high altitude area, you should use the finest and most accurate thermometer you can possibly obtain. In extreme cases it will pay to use a laboratory thermometer, rather than a candy thermometer. The difficulty of handling this short, clipless laboratory instrument may be overcome in many different ways.

Perhaps the simplest method of adapting it to candymaking use is to fasten it to the scale of your candy thermometer. This can be done by drilling four small holes through the candy thermometer base, thus: First, drill two holes alongside the glass tube of the candy thermometer, one about an inch from the bottom or lower end, and the second hole about an inch from the top. Now place the laboratory thermometer alongside the holes and mark the location for the other two holes directly opposite the first two. Drill the holes and then cut two short lengths of soft copper wire and run them through the holes at each end to hold the thermometer in place, paralleling the candy thermometer, and as nearly as possible directly opposite the same temperature marks so that you can watch the different readings obtained at the various temperatures. Twist the wires together at the back of the candy thermometer plate to secure the laboratory thermometer, but use great care to twist them only tightly enough to support it firmly, not so tightly as to snap the brittle glass tube.

However, it is probable that you will not have to go to such lengths, particularly if you purchase your candy thermometer locally and inquire if it is accurate for your area. Or you may be able to use it merely by making the adjustment in temperature called for in the recipe as adapted to your locale.

GLOSSARY

BLOOM: The streaking that results on chocolates if they are subjected to too high temperatures or to dampness. Also a term used to describe the strength of gelatin.

BONBON: A candy made from rich fondant, and coated with another kind of fondant, usually colored in pastels, or left white.

BONBON DOCTOR: The mixture of chemicals added to bonbon coating to impart a higher gloss.

BONBON FORK: The wire tool used for dipping bonbons.

CANDY CUP: The brown, white, or colored paper cups used for holding individual pieces of candy.

CENTERS: The insides of chocolate creams, made usually from fondant.

CHOCOLATE JIMMIES: Chocolate rice.

CHOCOLATE RICE: Small shreds of chocolate used for decorating candies and cakes.

CHOCOLATE SPRINKLES: Chocolate rice.

COCOA BUTTER: The fatty residue obtained in the processing of chocolate. Cocoa butter is used as a thinning medium for enrobing chocolate.

CORDIALLING: The term used to describe the liquifying process inside cordialled cherries.

CRINKLE CUPS: The paper cups used for holding chocolate creams or bonbons.

CROWN: The decorative ridge put on the tops of bonbons when dipping them with a bonbon fork.

CRYSTALLIZING: The process in which candy is covered with a layer of fine sugar crystals, in order to finish the candy, and keep it fresh for a longer period of time.

DECORETTES: A trade name for chocolate rice.

DEPOSITING: The term given to the making of candy wafers or molded forms when made with a depositing funnel and stick.

DEPOSITING FUNNEL: The tool used for depositing.

DIPPING: The term commonly used for enrobing or coating chocolates. Also used to describe the coating of bonbons.

DIPPING FORK: A wire tool used for dipping chocolates. Also, a bonbon fork.

DIPPING BOARD: A piece of thin plywood, masonite or corrugated cardboard, cut to the same size as a dipping paper, used to hold the paper when making chocolates.

DIPPING PAPER: The specially glazed paper on which to place dipped chocolates. The surface permits easy removal of the hardened chocolate.

DOCTORING: A term used to describe the process of imparting a gloss to bonbon coating.

DRAGEE: Silver or gold balls used in decorating candies. Also tiny white balls used in making commercial nonpareils.

ENROBING: The proper term for dipping chocolates.

FONDANT: The cooked creamy material from which the centers of chocolates and bonbons are made.

FONDANT KNIFE: The blade with which fondant is worked on the marble slab.

FUNNEL STICK: The stick used as a valve with the depositing funnel.

HARD-CRACK: That kind of candy which is cooked to a high temperature, and which hardens into a glassy mass. Used for lollipops and clear toys.

HARD-CRACK GLOVES: Pulling gloves.

HOLIDAYS: Spots left uncoated when dipping chocolates or bonbons.

LIQUOR: The commercial name for bitter dipping chocolate.

MACAROON COCONUT: A very finely shredded coconut used in candymaking and baking.

MOLD: In confectionery, the rubber molds used for depositing cream wafers, or the metal molds used for lollipops and clear toys.

PULLING GLOVES: The heavy leather gloves used for handling hot brittles.

SCRAPER: A fondant knife.

SEEDING: The starting of the crystallizing process by introducing a foreign body in to the syrup, the foreign body being the candy being crystallized, in our case.

SHELF LIFE: The term used to designate the length of time a candy will remain fresh before it is consumed.

SLAB: The piece of marble upon which most candy is made.

SLAB SCRAPER: A fondant knife.

SLAB OIL: Mineral oil.

SPATULA: A fondant knife in candymaking parlance.

SPRINKLES: Chocolate rice.

STRINGING: The term used to describe the laying of a string of chocolate on the tops of creams, when they are coated. Stringing is used both as a decoration, and an identification of the flavor of the piece.

SUGAR FLOWER: The different-sized flowers made from colored sugar paste. Used for cake and candy decoration.

SUGARING OUT: The term used to describe the turning of a hard-crack fondant into a sugary solid. Actually, a crystallizing process.

TEMPERING: As applied to chocolate, the method of conditioning the chocolate for proper dipping temperature.

INDEX

NOTE: Recipes appear with initial letters capitalized.